UNDERSTANDING PORNOGRAPHY AND SEXUAL ADDICTION

A RESOURCE FOR LDS FAMILIES AND LEADERS

Prepared by

S.A. LIFELINE
FOUNDATION

Published by Forward Press Publishing
San Antonio, TX

SA Lifeline Foundation is a non-profit 501(c)3 organization
committed to providing hope, support, education, and resources
for those impacted by pornography and sexual addiction. SA
Lifeline Foundation is not affiliated with any religion or any
organization. This publication is neither sponsored nor endorsed
by The Church of Jesus Christ of Latter-day Saints.

SA Lifeline Foundation makes this book available with
no motive of profit. Proceeds from the distribution of this
manual will be used to support the work of the Foundation,
delivering information and a message of hope that recovery
from pornography addiction is possible. This document is also
available online at no cost in printable PDF format at www.
salifeline.org. We ask that you share this resource manual as
widely as possible. In doing so, you will assist in the work of
bringing key knowledge and understanding about pornography
and sexual addiction to those who now suffer silently and those
who can best help them.

Front Cover: *Journey's End*, by Derek Hegsted, used with
permission. This powerful image of a man being embraced by
Christ is a depiction of the power of the Atonement and the joy
and peace of repentance.

Note: Throughout this manual, masculine pronouns have been
used when referring to those struggling with pornography. This
was employed for the sake of simplicity and readability and is
not intended to suggest that this is only a male problem. Women
increasingly use and become addicted to pornography.

Acknowledgments

This book is a compilation of information that represents thousands of hours of research and writing from many individuals, both professionals in the field of sexual addiction and non-professionals. All have extensive experience and expertise on the subject of pornography and sexual addiction. SA Lifeline Foundation wishes to express heartfelt thanks to those who have helped produce this manual.

Special thanks to: Steven and Rhyll Croshaw; Laurel Rogers; Alisa Rogers, JD; Linda Curley Christensen; Deseret Media Companies; Jeff Ford, LMFT; Daniel Gray, LCSW; Katie Gustafson; David Handy, JD; Toni Handy; Derek Hegsted; Donald L. Hilton Jr., MD; Craig L. Israelsen, PhD; Rod W. Jeppsen, LPC; Jill C. Manning, PhD; Todd and Jill Moulton, Greg Pearson, CPA; James A. Pixton, JD.; Karen Porter; John and Naomi Riding; Geoff Steurer, MS, LMFT; Kay Sumsion, RN; H. Dennis Tolley, PhD; Ann Tolley, JD; and Kathy Whitaker, RN.

Editorial staff: Bryan Crockett, Dan Hogan, Ed Brinton, Jonathan and Rachel Reddoch, Caitlin Schwanger, Karrae Brunner, and Jessika Speer.

Foreword

Do Not Despair for There Is Hope

H. Dennis Tolley, PhD

Given the rampant spread of pornography, it is easy to feel helpless against apparently overwhelming odds. The children of Israel faced a similar sense of hopelessness in the Book of 2 Kings.[1] A Syrian king had invaded Israel. When Elisha's servant arose one morning and looked out over the city wall, he saw the multitudes of enemy soldiers surrounding the city and was overcome by fear. He felt certain that Elisha would be captured and killed once the city walls were breached. When Elisha saw the army and the servant's fear, however, he spoke powerful words of faith and hope: "Fear not: for they that be with us are more than they that be with them."[2]

Elisha knew that God was on their side and that the Almighty's hosts were far more powerful than any earthly army. At Elisha's request, the veil was taken from the servant's eyes and he saw an angelic army—a multitude of horses and chariots of fire awaiting the Lord's bidding. God granted the servant a gift to see "the more" "that be with us."

The plague of pornography has become an intense worldwide war between good and evil. The very souls of God's children are the prize. When we see the expansive scope of this plague, it is easy to feel that we are but few and that anything we do is too little, too late.

Because pornography has now entered even the homes of the very righteous, it is tempting to surrender to an overwhelming sense of despair. But the scriptures and the prophets have told us clearly who will win this war. In the face of seemingly unbounded adversity, we need to remember that the Lord's armies are fighting beside us.

We are doing God's will; we will prevail. As we take active measures to become educated, protect ourselves, strengthen our homes, and appropriately help others, we will receive the help we need. "They that be with us are more than they that be with them."

1: *2 Kings 6*
2: *2 Kings 6:16*

The Game Has Changed

Donald L. Hilton Jr., MD

Even though airplanes had been used in World War I, the United States seriously underestimated the ability of air power in combat in the decades that followed. On December 7, 1941, at 7:02 a.m., at a small radar station on the northern side of the island of Oahu, Privates Joseph McDonald and George Elliott noticed a large group of planes approaching from the north. They told Lieutenant Kermit Tyler about the planes. When questioned by another soldier at headquarters, Lieutenant Tyler responded, "Well, don't worry about it. It's nothing." At 7:55 a.m., the bombing of Pearl Harbor began.[1] Air power thrust the United States into World War II at Pearl Harbor and effectively ended the war four years later when B-29s dropped the first atomic bombs on Japan. In this sense, air power was a game changer. Today, wars are fought differently, with jets, ballistic missiles, and remote-controlled drones playing key roles in military planning and execution.

Pornography, which is visual, aural, or written material intended to incite sexual desire, is today's game changer. It was present in ancient Egypt and Rome. Several recent developments, however, have changed the acceptance, nature, and delivery of pornography. Internet pornography in particular has become a game changer. It has been marketed as an acceptable pastime frowned on only by religious prudes. Today, what once would have been shocking is commonly accepted.

In his book *The Brain That Changes Itself*, Dr. Norman Doidge, a neurologist at Columbia, describes how pornography causes a rewiring of the neural circuits. The brain center that controls impulsiveness becomes supercharged, and the brain center for willpower shrinks. Those who have struggled with drug or alcohol addictions, as well as pornography addiction report that pornography was the hardest addiction for them to overcome.

Bill Margold, a male pornography star, said, "I'd like to really show what I believe the men want to see: violence against women. I firmly believe that we serve a purpose by showing that."[2] Given that young males ages twelve to seventeen are the main group[3] viewing pornography, we as a society have allowed Margold and his co-conspirators to become the de facto sexuality instructors for the upcoming generations.[4]

It is time we realize that we are blindly allowing another airstrike on our nation. The assault is hitting us on all fronts: cultural, moral, political, and biological. Internet pornography is a stealth attack on our homes and families through invisibly transmitted electrons. Education about the addictive, destructive nature of this attack is paramount, and hence the need for this manual. We must address prevention and recovery with the same tenacity the pornography industry has employed to invade our homes and our lives. Only then can we turn the tide and begin to win this war.

1: Walter Lord, Day of Infamy, *Henry Holt and Company, 1957, 1985, p 41-45.*

2: Gail Dines, Pornland: How Porn Has Hijacked Our Sexuality, *Beacon Press, Boston, 2010, xxvi.*

3: *http://www.safefamilies.org/sfStats.php*

4: G.M. Hald; N.M. Malamuth, C. Yuen. *"Pornography and attitudes supporting violence against women: revisiting the relationship in nonexperimental studies."* Aggression and Behavior, *2010; 36:14-20.*

Contents

Section

1 Introduction 1
    Considerations for Parents 2
    Considerations for Leaders 7

2 Understanding the Basics 17

3 Discussing Pornography 25
    Discussion Points for Children 25
    Discussion Points for Teens 26
    Discussion Points for Young Single Adults 27
    Discussion Points for Adults 29

4 Common Questions and Answers 33

5 Personal Stories 73
    Sitting in a Rowboat Throwing Marbles at a Battleship 73
    Would We React Differently to Cancer? 80
    Discovering Hope and Healing, Part I and II 82
    Finding the Power to Forgive 85
    Finding Myself 86
    Discussing Pornography as a Family 87

6 Articles 91
    The Effect of Pornography on the Spouse of an Addict 91
    Talking to Youth and Children about Pornography 94
    Creating a Safe Place to Talk about Dangerous Things 98
    Can Pornography Use Become an Actual Brain Addiction? . . . 101

7 Sample Lessons 107
    Lesson A: Our Bodies Are Special Gifts (Children Ages 4–11) 108
    Lesson B: Teaching about Pornography (Youth Ages 12–18) 113
    Lesson C: Discussing Pornography (Youth Ages 12–18) 117
    Lesson D: Developing Christlike Relationships That Lead to Marriage
             (Young Single Adults Ages 16–30) 122
    Lesson E: Replacing Fear with Faith (General Audience) 127

8 Handouts, Common Terms 133

9 Resources 147

10 Bibliography 150

IN LIGHT *of the prevalence of pornography addiction, a group of professionals, therapists, and concerned individuals have created this manual. Its purpose is to provide ready access to important information concerning pornography so that parents and leaders can be prepared to address the topic effectively, as directed by the Spirit.*

Traditionally there has been an assumption that good LDS people do not struggle with pornography. Bishops and stake presidents who openly address this problem find that there are many men and women in their wards and stakes who are adversely affected by pornography. Even more are affected by loved ones' use of pornography. It is a problem that must be addressed effectively and assertively.

> *"Now the corrupting influence of pornography, produced and disseminated for commercial gain, is sweeping over our society like an avalanche of evil. Here, brethren, I must tell you that our bishops and our professional counselors are seeing an increasing number of men involved with pornography, and many of those are active members."*
>
> — ELDER DALLIN H. OAKS
> *"Pornography," Ensign,* May 2005, p 87

As a parent or leader, your ability to help others is based on:

- Your awareness and understanding of pornography and sexual addiction.

- Your effectiveness in educating those around you about pornography addiction—how to safeguard against it, how to recognize it, and how to guide those affected to find help and healing.

- Your readiness to help individuals access the appropriate resources necessary for recovery and healing, including appropriate 12-Step recovery programs and professional counseling—both for the addicts and their spouse or loved ones.

In the address referenced above, Elder Oaks states:

> *"Pornography is...addicting. It impairs decision-making capacities and it 'hooks' its users, drawing them back obsessively for more and more. Pornography impairs one's ability to enjoy a normal emotional, romantic, and spiritual relationship with a person of the opposite sex. It erodes the moral barriers that stand against inappropriate, abnormal, or illegal behavior."*

Because people, situations, and available resources vary greatly, there is no single, most effective way to address this problem. It requires each parent or leader to prayerfully determine the appropriate course of action as guided by the Lord. Use this manual and the resources cited in this manual to arm yourselves with knowledge. The battle against pornography is a battle for the very souls of mankind, and God will give you the guidance and courage you need to help Him in this fight.

Introduction

Considerations for Parents

Children and teens are being bombarded with falsehoods about gender roles, sex, love, and procreation. Elder Boyd K. Packer said, "Failing to teach and to warn and to discipline is to destroy."[1] Sexuality is sacred. It is important that parents not abdicate their responsibility to actively teach children regarding healthy sexuality, as well as its counterfeit – pornography.

For many children, teens, and young adults, their main education about sexuality comes from their peers, TV, and movies, and from viewing pornography. This education is devoid of a value system and makes no connection between sexuality and honesty, commitment, compassion, empathy, and selflessness. It is human sexuality devoid of human intimacy, the exact opposite of God's divine plan.

Many parents worry that discussing sexual topics plainly and boldly might trigger curiosity and encourage experimentation. However, when parents openly discuss sexual topics in an age-appropriate way, youth are less likely to experiment and are more likely to remain abstinent.

Parents should take active measures to limit their children's exposure to pornography by installing Internet filters, placing computers in safe locations, establishing clear standards for media use as a family, and not allowing cell phones or computers in bedrooms at night. But parents must remember that, even with these precautions, they cannot fully protect their children against pornography exposure.

As parents become educated, teach their children, and seek the Lord's guidance, they can help protect their homes from pornography. They can also help their children gain a healthy perspective that will enable them to walk away from this addictive material when they are exposed to it.

External monitoring will not be sufficient to protect children from pornography. In addition parents must teach children correct principles and healthy sexuality to build moral conviction in order to help them develop a sense of internal monitoring.

Parents must teach:

- Healthy sexuality

- Marriage-centered chastity

- The importance of avoiding pornography

- The need for open discussion about experiences with pornography

- Consequences of improper sexuality

- Benefits of sexual restraint[1]

1: Jason Carroll, PhD

1: "Ye are the Temple of God," Ensign, Nov. 2000, p 72-74.

The following are specific actions parents can take to combat this problem:

◈ Have regular talks with your children, teens, and young adults in which you discuss healthy sexuality, marriage-centered chastity, and their exposure to pornography. You might start the first talk with, *"I remember the first time I saw pornography; tell me about your first time."* Then follow up this talk with regular discussions.

◈ Be informed. Teach your children, teens, and young adults about the physical, emotional, and social dangers of pornography—not just the spiritual dangers.

◈ Read *He Restoreth My Soul*, by Donald L. Hilton Jr., MD, and *What's the Big Deal About Pornography?* by Jill C. Manning, PhD.

◈ Watch the videos on the SA Lifeline website (www.salifeline.org):

  ✦ *Safeguarding Teens and Young Adults from Pornography,* Jason Carrol, PhD

  ✦ *Pornography and Its Effects on the Brain,* Donald L. Hilton Jr., MD

  ✦ *Preparing for Healthy Intimacy – A Message for Young Single Adults,* Jill C. Manning, PhD. and Dan Gray, LCSW

  ✦ See pages 147–149 for additional resources.

◈ Become active in organizations that are fighting against pornography, such as:

  ✦ SA Lifeline Foundation
    www. salifeline.org

  ✦ Utah Coalition Against Pornography
    www. utahcoalition.org

  ✦ Fight the New Drug
    www.fightthenewdrug.org

  ✦ Pornography Harms
    www.pornharms.com

> *As our children grow, they need information taught by parents more directly and plainly about what is and is not appropriate. Parents need to teach children to avoid any pornographic photographs or stories. Talk to them plainly about sex. Let this information come from parents in the home in an appropriate way.*
>
> **— ELDER M. RUSSELL BALLARD**
> "Like a Flame Unquenchable," *Ensign,* May 1999, p 85

Introduction

Beautiful Gift, Ugly Package

A Mother of a Recovering Sexual Addict
Shares Hope

My husband and I first discovered our middle son, then age twelve, had a pornography problem when we were getting our computer fixed. I had asked the technician to look for pornography evidence. I felt shocked, angry, worried, and confused. We had a home where we had consistently taught the importance of a relationship with God and right from wrong. We had held regular family home evenings, family scripture study, etc. We had strong standards about appropriate media, had the computer in a well-trafficked area, and had established family limits on electronic devices. We, at times, taught about sex in positive ways. It had not been enough.

We confronted our son together later that night. At first he denied it, but then admitted it. We asked more questions and he started to cry. His strongest reaction came when I asked him how many times he had looked at pornography. Finally he confessed to "over thirty times." I suspected this meant even more. I felt compassion for him and knew he needed to know that we still loved him, and that we would help him. We installed a strict Internet filter, talked about the damaging effects of pornography, and he promised he was done with it.

I was uneducated, so I believed him. We went forward with our family life, struggling through the something-is-not-right feeling. As time went on, I kept thinking his impulsivity, shyness, feelings of entitlement, anger, blaming, lying, withholding truth, lack of self-care, shutting down emotionally, lack of empathy, and instigating personality were just his weaknesses. Or maybe they were part of being a teenager. Sometimes when he was disciplined for doing something, almost immediately he would do it again, and my husband and I would scratch our heads and wonder why he didn't get it and if he was just not very bright? On the contrary, he seemed plenty smart,

but there were areas where he did not seem to be able to put two and two together.

Looking back, I can see all these elements were outgrowths of his addiction. He just could not control his impulses because of the damage the addiction had caused his brain. Like other addicts, he often unconsciously tried to do things to make his loved ones angry so he had an excuse to act out.

A couple of years went by. One afternoon I caught him masturbating and looking at pornography while I was in the same room. He thought he could hide it. As I confronted him, I was incredulous. I knew then he had a serious problem if he was desperate enough to act out under these conditions. I told him I thought he had an addiction and talked to him about what that was. I explained that he would need to tell other people about his problem so he could get help. Addiction means there is no way you can overcome it on your own.

My husband was the bishop at the time, and so he started meeting with our son regularly and gave him the Church's 12-Step booklet. They had many great talks about shoring yourself up spiritually, and my husband asked for regular accountability from my son. Because I knew my husband was working with him in an ecclesiastical role, and that meant confidentiality, I didn't think I could be a part of that issue any more.

The other side effects of the addiction continued, such as lying, impulsivity, and high demand for entertainment and adrenaline-producing activities. I still did not know these were related to the pornography. I tried to love and guide him, disciplining him for hurting his younger brothers, and not tolerating disrespectful attitudes. When consequences didn't seem to be helping the behaviors much, I'd try a different approach of more loving compliments and appreciation. I made gratitude lists for everything he was doing right, so I wouldn't be frustrated or judgmental. Occasionally at church I noticed he was not taking the sacrament, so I knew he still was having problems, but I continued to tell myself that my husband was working with him, it was part of what a lot of young men are tempted by in their youth. I was in denial.

Then toward the end of our son's junior year, when he was sixteen, my husband felt a strong spiritual impression to read the texts on my son's phone. There we discovered that he was making out for the purpose of becoming sexually aroused. He confessed to lying to my husband for some time about continuing to look at pornography, and had minimized his true masturbation habits. It was then we all woke up to the fact that this was a serious addiction that was not going to go away with willpower, teaching, or even spiritual interventions alone.

By the grace of God, we found a therapist qualified in pornography and sexual addiction. My husband and I attended weekly sessions with our son for a month. Because finances and time were tight, my husband attended the 12-Step group S-Anon, my son attended his own 12-Step group and group therapy, and I attended my counseling group. We discontinued individual sessions. Hope was high, but progress was slow.

After an initial honeymoon period where he seemed willing to do whatever was necessary to get freed from addiction, my son realized recovery was really hard work and started to drag his feet. My husband and I did not always agree about what the best course of action was with our son's needs, and since I was in therapy alone, we were on different learning curves. Periods of seeming "recovery" were followed by confessions of acting out and more lies. Because my son was a minor, there are complexities and confusion that adults in recovery do not have to navigate. Some helpful responses in working with a child in recovery would be considered over managing recovery for an adult addict. Many weeks felt like we took two steps forward, but one and a half steps back. If my son was doing well, I was flying high with hope and peace.

When he struggled, I was in the depths of despair and anxiety. I call this "riding his rollercoaster." When he was up, I was up. If he was down, I was down.

Curiously, gifts for me started to unfold. Through counseling I was able to learn how to take care of myself and get off my son's rollercoaster. I was awakened to things about myself that I never would have become conscious of without having to wrestle addiction in my home. For example, I never would have realized how much I felt I could not trust others to help with my needs. I've learned specifics about our weaknesses as parents that contributed to the situation. I now have permission to make mistakes and take responsibility for them—it's part of life for everyone. I am more comfortable in my own skin. I know that whatever I'm feeling is okay, that I have truth, and I can share it in a healthy way. I feel more comfortable in social settings and can see the greatness in others.

I feel peace and serenity no matter what my son is doing or not doing because I can more truthfully recognize my responsibility and leave the rest up to God. I now trust God completely to do His part. I know how to hold boundaries that are motivated by truth, love, and clarity about what my son is capable of managing. I used to think I was responsible to fix my son, and other people for that matter. This made me feel so burdened and frustrated. I always knew God loved me, but now I know He loves me for just being me, not because of anything I do, serve, sacrifice, or accomplish. I love knowing He wants to give me things and help me be happy right now, as well as in the long run.

A precious gift is knowing in my bones that anything that happens to me can be consecrated for my gain, that nothing can really hurt me. God is always there for me, and I am safe in his hands.

I can see through to other people's shame and damaged spirits more often and feel compassion, not judgment or offense. I feel a new confidence in my daily priorities and that all this growth is a process; I don't have to know everything right now. I feel balance and patience. Ironically, addiction, though ugly, keeps giving me gifts in recovery for which I am so grateful. It was such an overwhelming adversity that there was no way my puny human effort stood a chance to fight it. Turning to that majestic, loving Power greater than myself has given me a priceless gift of a deeper relationship with my Savior and the trust, hope, and security I feel in His care.

If there were nothing else, the gifts I have received would be payment enough. Happily, there is more. My son has made wonderful progress. He continues to fight the fight and never gives up. His recovery is still progressing, and we don't always know if he stands on solid ground yet. He is more open with his feelings, his struggles, and his triumphs. I feel like I am starting to know the real, great soul he is. All of the negative effects of the pornography addiction are subsiding. He is rarely blaming, or entitled, and when he is, he takes responsibility for it more often. He has started expressing gratitude, love, and an interest in his family members that previously did not exist.

He feels a tenderness and empathy toward suffering individuals now. He plans ahead and realizes the value of structure. He takes care of himself physically, educationally, and with his goals in a way we hadn't seen until the last six months. He can say he's sorry now. He can do it without berating himself or justifying. His relationship with me and my husband is closer, more connected, and more honest than it has ever been. He is more aware than most adults of his complete dependence on God, and he has had some soul searching times to commit to what kind of a man he wants to be. He's gaining an awareness of how his choices strengthen or damage relationships. He can examine motives for his behavior, and can stand up for what is true for him. He has recognized miracles big and little.

Do I wish we could have all these great blessings delivered in a different package than sexual addiction? Yes, definitely yes. But if that is the way it had to come to me, I'll take it. Truly, through the intense work of recovery, God is giving me beauty for ashes.

Considerations for Leaders

When interviewing teens and adults, bishops and stake presidents who ask, "When was the last time you viewed pornography?" have discovered that many members under their stewardship are currently struggling with this problem. When someone is viewing pornography, knows pornography is wrong, and has a sincere desire to quit, but still keeps going back to it, their viewing is no longer a choice but has become an addiction. The addiction damages the willpower center of the brain and feeds the impulsivity center.

Merely knowing that pornography is wrong and having a sincere desire to stop viewing is not sufficient to break this addiction. Pornography is an addiction that feeds on secrecy and shame and can destroy a person, body and soul. It damages the individual's ability to emotionally connect to those around him. Spiritual healing, as well as emotional, psychological, and neurological healing, must take place. Leaders can play an important role in helping the addict find recovery in each of these areas by meeting with the person regularly. In addition, they can help him find a qualified sexual addiction counselor, an appropriate sexual addiction 12-Step group, and educational materials.

Pornography and sexual addiction have a devastating effect on the addict's spouse and other loved ones. Very rarely do spouses get adequate and appropriate help, support, or counseling. Leaders can be instrumental in making sure that the spouse, parents, or other loved ones of the addict receive the support they need by listening to their concerns, validating their experience, offering words of comfort, and providing information about where help is available, including educational materials.

Specific actions some leaders have taken to combat this problem include:

- Select and train one or more individuals to serve as specialists, coordinating training to educate others about pornography.

- Make presentations in ward councils, leadership meetings, Relief Society, priesthood, Young Women and Young Men groups.

- Regularly meet with those struggling with pornography and their spouses to promote consistent accountability, provide encouragement, and help facilitate the repentance and healing process.

- Make available brochures, books, and other educational resources relating to pornography addiction and recovery. (See *Handout* and *Resource* sections of this manual.)

- Compile a list of effective 12-Step meetings, therapists, and other local resources, and help establish additional 12-Step support group meetings where needed.

- Become educated yourself. Read *He Restoreth My Soul* by Donald L. Hilton, Jr., MD, *What's the Big Deal About Pornography?* by Jill C. Manning, PhD, and *Lord, I Believe: Help Thou Mine Unbelief*, by Rod W. Jeppsen, MC, LPC, CSAT.

Pornography thrives where there is shame and secrecy. When we gain knowledge about the spiritual, physical, emotional, and social destruction caused by pornography, we can teach better. By learning to recognize pornography addiction and understand the steps to recovery, we can win this war, one soul at a time.

Introduction

Don't Fix It

A Former Bishop Shares His Experience

As a man, as a father, and as a bishop, I've had plenty of experience trying to solve problems. It's almost ingrained in me—fix it. When something breaks, something needs to be done. If someone is suffering, I want to help. If you're a Church leader, it's likely been deeply instilled in you that you have a solemn responsibility to do everything within your power to assist those in need and bring peace to those that are hurting. And then you have someone who comes to you asking for help with an addiction. And you can't fix it.

I've struggled together with members of my congregation who suffer from pornography addiction. They come in genuinely repentant, seeking help and guidance. I give my very best counsel and they go forward with a new conviction—a new conviction that lasts a few months at most and sometimes only a few days.

The purpose of this letter is to give you a lot of hope and a little direction, because in addition to working from a bishop's standpoint, I'm also the father of a boy who has been addicted to pornography and masturbation. I met with him as his priesthood leader and wanted to help more than anything. I wanted to fix it, and I believe I was wrong for taking that approach. I offer two suggestions for you to consider as an ecclesiastical leader.

First, Moses 1:39 states, "This is *my* work and *my* glory—to bring to pass the immortality and eternal life of man" [emphasis added]. It's *His* work, not yours. You and I are not ordained or set apart to take the place of God. We offer help and guidance and counsel and support. But the members of your congregation are God's children who have agency, and they must learn to access the Atonement of Jesus Christ if they are to be saved. You will not save them because you are not the Savior. Surrender your desire to save and let God do His work. Make that clear to your members.

And second, though you are not the one to offer salvation, you do have a unique position in a person's life. You can facilitate three things that help every addict in his recovery: (1) honesty, (2) responsibility and (3) humility. As a Church leader you can assist in these areas. But I believe the one where you will make the most difference will be with *humility*. Encourage the addict to be honest and responsible, but I encourage you to also help him to attend a 12-Step program and seek professional counseling. A sponsor and a therapist will help with regular opportunities for the addict to continue practicing responsibility and affirm his honesty. But as his spiritual leader, you will have a wonderful opportunity to teach humility and to help him find the Savior, which will bring him healing. Give him counsel and help him to be humble—but not humiliated. Share your own faith in the Savior and affirm your dependence on God. Never be shy to affirm your inadequacies, but don't apologize that you are only doing what you can. You are a spiritual leader doing all you can to point people to the Healer.

Don't carry the burden alone. Let each person perform his or her role. Counselors, 12-Step programs, family, and friends all contribute in important ways. Remember the most important role is that of the Savior, and the addict's relationship with the Savior is what will ultimately save him. Just do what you do best—give counsel and guidance to help him deepen his faith in the Lord Jesus Christ. And don't try to fix it.

What Can We Do Now to Stop the Progression of the Problem?

In his book, *He Restoreth My Soul*, Donald L. Hilton, Jr., MD says that we are currently "losing the war" on pornography. He then summarizes some keys to changing the direction of the pornography problem.

1. Treat pornography and sexual addiction as a full addiction and not from a behavioral or spiritual perspective alone.

2. Individuals struggling with pornography and sexual addiction must understand that because this is a true addiction, they will not be able to stop unless they seek help from appropriate sources.

3. Disclosure of each incident of viewing or sexually acting out to an appropriate priesthood leader and to the spouse is essential to obtain both repentance and recovery.

4. While we have emphasized prevention in the past, and should continue to do so, we must also recognize that virtually all of our young men and many of our young women are already seriously exposed.

5. Understand that many of young men returning from missions are slipping quickly into addiction, and we must be ready to support them with 12-Step support groups specific to pornography addiction immediately upon return from their mission.

6. Recognize that many married men are secretly addicted. It is important to have support groups ready to help them emerge from addiction.

7. We must provide support groups for the spouse who has been harmed by the pornography or sexual addiction of her husband.

8. Realize the importance of educating young women about the prevalence and tenacity of pornography addiction so they will understand and be fully informed as they enter the world of dating.

9. Educate and train leaders to understand addiction and the importance of addressing both repentance and recovery.

10. While professional individual, couples, and group therapy is integral for many to achieve long-term recovery, 12-Step support groups should be the backbone of recovery, as not all will have access to therapists experienced in treating sexual addiction.

 ◈ In addition, watch the videos on the SA Lifeline Foundation website (www.salifeline.org):

   ◆ *Myth: Marriage Cures a Pornography Problem*

   ◆ *Impact of Pornography*

   ◆ *Why the 12-Steps Are So Effective*

Letter from the Spouse of an Addict

Dear Bishop,

The women who have been affected by the addiction of a spouse are most often faithful covenant-keeping women. Because of the trauma associated with their situation, these women frequently question their own self-worth and even their testimonies. We cannot afford to lose these faithful sisters and mothers of the rising generation to the effects of this plague.

Please understand that my husband's problem is not in any way associated with my appearance or behavior. I did not cause and cannot change or fix my husband's addiction. My husband most likely developed this problem long before he knew me and because of his agency has chosen to act as he does. Please do not suggest that I just "need to love him more," and he will not act out. This only adds to the craziness that I already feel.

Help me to understand that I have been traumatized, and, with kindness and concern, help me to find resources to begin to heal. Having a person to talk with who has experience in these matters, a 12-Step group, and education about what I am dealing with will be helpful. I need someone who understands the magnitude of this problem and is able to hold my husband accountable for his actions. As our bishop, you can firmly, directly, and lovingly do so because of your concern for his spiritual welfare—and mine also.

Help me to feel safe. My confidence in priesthood leadership has been shaken because I believed all along that my husband was being true to his covenants, only to discover that he has been untrue to me. I need to believe that there is a kind and honest priesthood leader whom I can trust. Encourage me to slow down my life and my emotions and help me to have a glimmer of hope that the dream I have held so dear of a loving, eternal marriage can be realized with time and effort by both my husband and me.

In the meantime, help me to set and keep appropriate boundaries. These boundaries will help me to feel safe, while I learn that I truly am a beloved daughter of God. Through that knowledge, I can recognize my ability to make choices and find happiness through being true to Him and to myself.

Letter from an Addict

Dear Bishop,

Perhaps no other individual has greater potential to influence an addict in the direction of recovery than his local priesthood leader. Unfortunately, the opposite may also be true. If a leader fails to understand the magnitude of the disease and what is required for real recovery, vital opportunities to heal the heart and mind of the addict will have been lost. Compassion for the addict is rarely lacking. On the other hand, knowledge of what the addict needs to achieve true recovery often is.

Bishop, thank you so much for the love and compassion you demonstrate when you counsel with those of us suffering from sex and pornography addiction. As you know, this is a difficult and confusing affliction. We need your help to overcome it, and, once we have done so, we need your help to remain free from it. As a recovering addict, I implore you to keep a few things in mind.

First, please know that an addict cannot recover on his own even though he may believe he can. Someone struggling with the viewing of pornography or other unwanted sexual behavior is suffering from a compulsion every bit as strong as addiction to cocaine. To overcome his addiction, the addict needs help not only from you, his priesthood leader, but also from professional counselors or therapists, as well as the support of one or more addiction recovery groups.

Second, please understand that debilitating fear is burning in the heart and mind of the sex or pornography addict. I feel certain that if you polled the many LDS men currently suffering in silence, most would tell you that the three most important things in their life are their wife, their children, and the Church. The prospect of meeting with a priesthood leader to disclose this problem brings with it a fear that the addict may very well lose the only three things in this world that truly matter to him. The fear is all the more paralyzing for the unrecovered addict who has once again relapsed. Seeing his wife's anguished face and his children's fear and confusion, as well as possibly facing Church discipline are no minor obstacles to disclosure, repentance, and recovery. The fear is real, it is enormous, and it hurts like nothing else the addict has ever felt.

Third, in addition to fear, disclosure and reporting to a priesthood leader often engender shame and humiliation in the addict. Even though a leader may be compassionate and encouraging, an unrecovered addict cannot help but feel shame for repeatedly engaging in undesired but compulsive sexual behavior. He cannot help but feel humiliation each time he has to sit across the desk from his bishop and talk about whether he has been able to remain chaste since the last check-in. These feelings are present even if the report is positive. They are all the stronger and more painful if the report is negative.

(continued on next page)

Letter from an Addict (continued)

Fourth, please understand that the viewing of pornography is really just an outward manifestation of a more deep-rooted addiction to lust. What this means is that an addict who is currently abstaining from the viewing of pornography but is receiving no treatment for the addiction is most likely not in recovery. At best, he is "white knuckling," which means that he is abstaining by sheer will-power and not because he has achieved any lasting change in his behavior.

Fifth, dishonesty is a major component of the disease of addiction. Addicts seek to minimize or cover up the seriousness and extent of their acting out, often by lying both to themselves and to others. Addicts are in pain and spend a significant portion of their day trying to reduce that pain and medicate with their drug. Having to suffer once again through fear, shame, and humiliation can be more than an impaired addict believes he can bear, and so he lies. Fear, shame, and humiliation are three of the strongest negative emotions that can lead an unrecovered addict to act out again if he does not acquire the tools he needs to deal with them.

Bishop, I need you to help me get those tools. I need you to encourage me to seek therapy or counseling and to get involved in 12-Step recovery groups. I need you to help me understand the importance of becoming educated about pornography and sexual addiction. If I tell you that pornography or acting out sexually is "no longer a problem," I need you to kindly and patiently help me understand that addiction ebbs and flows like the ocean's tide. Although the compulsions may have subsided for a time, they will return. They always do, and when they do, I need recovery tools and support in place or I will fall again like I have so many times before. I need to learn it is not about "stopping" —because I have done that a thousand times. I need to learn how "not to start again."

Letter From the Daughter of a Recovering Sex Addict
Watching My Father's Transformation

I am the daughter of a recovering sex addict. My story isn't all that dramatic. I might even venture that in a peculiar way this challenge has been among one of the greatest blessings of my life. Given the option, I don't think I would have chosen of myself to pass over this mountain. However, the lessons I have learned as a result of this experience are proving to bless myself and family in unspeakable ways.

Growing up, I didn't feel differently than other children. In fact, I counted myself uniquely blessed. I was loved, well provided for, and had an abundance of opportunity to develop my interests and talents. I seemed to have a wellspring of confidence at my core. As a result I fared well in my pursuits academically and socially.

I recall feeling close to my mom through my formative years. She was my primary confidant and mentor. In contrast, I occasionally talked with my dad, but on a very superficial level and rarely sought him out for emotional support. This was mostly due to the fact that he was often working long hours or away on business. When he was home, he felt distant—rarely speaking of himself or engaging me in conversation about my activities and interests. In spite of this, I did believe he loved me and thought that my relationship with my dad was normal, even healthy.

As a young child, I have only vague recollections of challenges in my parents' marriage. Any issues they had were discussed behind closed doors. It wasn't until high school that I really began to see something amiss in my parents' relationship. I recall occasionally worrying about the prospect of my parents separating, but the feeling didn't linger. Full of grit, my mom was generally upbeat and positive. In my opinion she did a tremendous job of maintaining the household and keeping everything and everyone in order. Yet as I grew older and became more perceptive I noticed something weighed heavily on her. Finances were a constant concern during this period, but I felt there was something deeper causing her anxiety.

As I entered my older teen years and began interacting more with my friends' fathers, I noticed the level of warmth and emotional closeness some of them shared with their dads. It was then that I started to recognize how much was missing in my own father/daughter relationship. I didn't realize it at the time, but for many years I didn't know my father. In his shame-based Jekyll and Hyde life, he was limited in his ability to love and be loved.

In my concern, I began soliciting my mom for information so I could provide some emotional support. She would never go into detail about my father's behavior, but it soon became clear to me that Dad had a problem—the extent of which I didn't learn til later. The hardest thing for me at the time was seeing my mom suffer. She was clearly in pain and there was little I could do for her.

(continued on next page)

Section 1

Watching My Father's Transformation (continued)

I soon graduated from high school and moved away from home. Preoccupied with college and other activities I was home only occasionally and for a time was oblivious to the trouble brewing between my parents.

It all came to a head years later only months after I was married. It was a pleasant Sunday afternoon and just after we arrived at my parents' home, my dad ushered my husband and I outside, sat us down, and proceeded to tell us that he had just been excommunicated from the LDS church. He went into some detail about the actions that led up to him losing his membership. I was devastated. I felt anger, sadness, and a deep sense of betrayal.

Here is where the blessings began:

Despite the anger and sadness, I was able to put my arms around my dad, tell him I loved him, and forgive him. I credit myself a very little for this frank forgiveness. First, my father had demonstrated forgiveness and patience for me on previous occasions, softening my heart toward him. Second, the way my mom was choosing to deal with the situation diffused much of my own anger. She wasn't bitter and dramatic. She calmly sat next to him and through glossy eyes said that she was going to try and support my dad as he worked toward recovery of his addiction. I decided that if she could forgive him – one who had suffered so directly and deeply as a result of his choices – I could do as much. She did, however, make it clear that she wouldn't support him in his addiction if he continued to act out. I recall her saying that "she would see how things went" as my dad behaved in a way that could start rebuilding her trust. Finally and most importantly, I felt the power of the Atonement wash over me, enabling me to rise above the bitterness and shame that could have easily taken hold of my heart.

I won't pretend that all the anger and sadness was gone that day. As the days and weeks passed, there were times when those feelings would resurface and I would vent to my husband or petition my Heavenly Father for help as I waded through my grief and fear. Even though my dad was doing well in his recovery, I knew there weren't any guarantees for him or my parents' marriage. But on the whole, I marvel at how easily I was able to forgive and move forward. Doing so freed me from the debilitating effects of resentment, shame, and bitterness that have overcome some individuals in similar situations.

Over five years later, I look back and am grateful for the lessons I have learned through this experience. I have learned not to be so afraid of this issue. I know as a mother I will deal with this in some form with my own children. Yet I feel like I can face

(continued on next page)

Watching My Father's Transformation (continued)

this problem with courage because I have the education, tools, and a testimony of the Atonement to help me through. I know recovery from pornography and sex addiction is possible. I have witnessed it! In watching my father's transformation, I have seen the Atonement's power reach farther and deeper than I ever thought possible. I used to be so black and white in my thinking, certain that if I or others messed up, that was it. There was no going back. But I have since realized that such thinking denies the redemptive power of the Atonement and its supreme power to heal hearts and change the repentant. Understanding this truth helps me to be more patient and forgiving of my own weaknesses as well as others' weaknesses because I know the Atonement works if only we will accept its power.

My father has worked tirelessly over the past several years to stay on the road of recovery. He is doing remarkably well and in the process is helping many others with this issue. Recovery is a daily effort for anyone battling through this difficulty. It is at times a challenge for both my parents as they continue to work toward recovery as individuals and as a couple. But through their faith and steady effort, they are growing together each day and are happier in their marriage and healthier as individuals than I have ever seen them.

Understanding the Basics

THIS SECTION PROVIDES A SUMMARY *of key information relating to pornography addiction. The "Frequently Asked Questions" and "Discussing Pornography with Others" sections provide more detailed information. Many are surprised and concerned to find that their neighbors, friends, and family members are those who are struggling with pornography addiction. Those who need help may include successful businessmen, returned missionaries, individuals married in the temple, or members serving in Church leadership positions. Because of shame and a fear of devastating consequences if they are found out, most who are struggling with pornography keep their behavior a secret.*

What is Pornography and Sexual Addiction?

Pornography is material that is sexually explicit and that has the primary intended purpose of sexual arousal.[1] Pornography addiction is a sub-category of sexual addiction and is progressive. It typically starts out with occasionally looking at pictures of scantily dressed people and then progresses from softcore to hardcore pornography. This progression can lead to acting out behaviors such as online and in-person emotional and sexual affairs, visiting strip clubs, and soliciting prostitutes.

If someone is addicted to alcohol, he would be strongly advised to seek counseling and immediately begin attending Alcoholics Anonymous meetings. It is essential to recognize that use of pornography, like alcohol, can lead to addiction. As with addiction to drugs or alcohol, it cannot be conquered through willpower alone.

Common advice may sound like, "You have a problem with pornography? Just make up your mind not to view it anymore, stick to your commitments, think pure thoughts, read your scriptures, and pray more." While all those suggestions are important spiritual activities, they do not represent the complete recovery pathway for addressing a pornography

addiction problem. Pornography addiction is a physical addiction that chemically alters the brain. To treat this addiction, serious measures are required, including a substantial amount of outside professional help.[2]

A common misconception is that a compulsion to view pornography will disappear following marriage. While marriage may temporarily halt the use of pornography by disrupting the pattern of the addiction, the compulsion generally resurfaces and escalates. Pornography is often used as a way to deal with negative emotions and to cope with life's problems, just like alcohol or illicit drugs. Although pornography use is not as common among women, the number of women viewing pornography is increasing rapidly.

Defining the Problem

Pornography is a rampant problem in our society. Studies suggest that 70% of men ages 18 to 34 visit pornography websites in a typical month[3], and 47% of families in the United States say pornography is a problem in their home.[4] A survey conducted in 2008 found that nearly 9 out of 10 (87%) young men and

---

1: Jill C. Manning, PhD, What's the Big Deal About Pornography? *(2008)* Shadow Mountain Press, Salt Lake City, UT.

2: For additional information, see the chart in *Handout* section of this manual, *"Contrasting Healthy Sexuality and Pornographic Portraits of Sexuality."*

3: *http://www.sync-blog.com/sync/2010/06/internet-porn-stats-should-parents-be-concerned.html*

4: *http://www.safefamilies.org/sfStats.php*

nearly one third (31%) of young women reported using pornography.[5] The average age at which children first see online pornography is 11.[6] Although statistics are not specifically available for the LDS population, it is estimated they are similar.

Pornography use is almost always carefully hidden. Directly asking about pornography viewing can open important discussions. An easy way to determine if an individual has a possible addiction is if they tell themselves that they are not going to look at pornography anymore and then find themselves doing it anyway. A teen may not have the same deep addiction that someone with 35 years of struggle has, but both persons need to take the addiction seriously.

Because pornography is so rampant, it is important to provide training and education for everyone. Openness does not mean condoning behavior or lessening consequences. It means eliminating the secrecy surrounding this subject and helping people understand that the use of pornography is widespread and needs to be openly addressed in an appropriate manner.

The Effects of Pornography on the Spouse and Marriage

When a wife discovers her husband's pornography use, the emotions experienced are similar to the grieving process associated with the death of a loved one: shock, disbelief or denial, anger, and depression. Many women will experience post-tramatic stress disorder and suffer greatly. Acknowledging, accepting, and allowing those feelings to take their course is important. Pornography frequently changes the addict's personality, influences the way he treats and interacts with others, and causes an emotional distance from those around him. The afflicted spouse often feels betrayed, rejected, abandoned, and unimportant. Deep loneliness and feeling responsible for the spouse's addiction are almost universal. Anger at the addicted spouse and even toward God is common. "I did everything I was supposed to do. Is this what I get

for it?" Spouses may feel abandoned not only physically and emotionally, but also spiritually.

Pornography addicts frequently pressure their spouses to keep the issue private. This isolation compounds the downward spiral of unhealthy feelings and counter-productive behavior. Without appropriate help and counseling, the emotional, physical, and spiritual health of the spouse will deteriorate.[7]

Pornography use may eventually lead to divorce. Statistically, 55% of divorces are related to pornography.[8] Nevertheless, a large number of couples are able to find recovery and healing through recognition of this addiction and by seeking appropriate help. Several factors influence the probability of healing the relationship. (For more information, see the chart in the Handout section, "Am I Making Effective Changes to Deal with My Spouse's Addiction?" and "Am I Serious About Dealing with My Pornography Problem?")

⬧ The addict chooses to get appropriate help, including receiving counseling from a qualified sexual addiction counselor and participating in a 12-Step sexual addiction program.

⬧ The couple has realistic expectations. Change takes time and there will often be relapses. With good counseling and support, however, these slips become less severe and less frequent.

5: http://www.safefamilies.org/sfStats.php

6: Jerry Roplato, *Internet Pornography Statistics,* http://internet-filter-review. toptenreviews.com/internet-pornography-statistics.html

7: For more information, see the chart "Recovery and Healing From the Effects of Pornography Addiction."

8: Jill C. Manning, PhD, 2006, *Impact of Internet Pornography on Marriage and the Family: A Review of the Research. Sexual Addiction and Compulsivity, Vol. 13, 233-249*

♦ Restoring a healthy relationship is much more probable if both the addicted individual and the afflicted spouse get qualified counseling, participate in 12-Step support groups, meet regularly with their bishop, and study appropriate educational materials.

♦ Many counselors recommend not making any permanent or major life decisions for at least a year. Over time, trust can be rebuilt and the relationship can heal if both partners are willing to do their part.

> The person engaging in the behavior is the **addict**. Because of the depth of the trauma experienced, we refer to the addict's spouse as being **afflicted**.

The Road to Recovery

Recovery from pornography addiction is difficult, but attainable. Those who are completely committed to doing what it takes to find and maintain recovery will be successful. Recovery involves:

♦ Desiring to recover and honestly admitting to others the magnitude of the problem.

♦ Becoming educated about the nature of pornography addiction and the recovery process.

♦ Creating a safe environment where triggers and temptations are less likely to occur.

♦ Continued participation in a 12-Step recovery program.

♦ Seeking professional counseling. This will usually include a mixture of individual counseling, couples therapy, and group counseling (at least 18 months is typically required).

♦ Seeking spiritual help by counseling with an ecclesiastical leader as well as seeking inspiration directly from Heavenly Father and applying the power of the Atonement of Jesus Christ.

Abstinence is not the same as *recovery*. Abstinence involves going a period of time without viewing pornography. Recovery requires a lifestyle change and involves relearning healthy sexuality, resetting unhealthy expectations, and establishing positive patterns of interaction with others. Recovering individuals must learn to manage emotions, stress, relationships, and other factors that underlie their addictive behaviors. They must learn to differentiate between lust and healthy love.

> The acronym **HALT** is a reminder of conditions that make us more susceptible to relapse:
>
> **Hungry:** With many of us, an agitated state of mind—haste, hurry, or "hyper," for example—seems at least as perilous as hunger. And hunger itself can lead to binge eating, as many of us so well know. Binging on food can trigger the sexual addiction.
>
> **Angry:** Anger, resentment, and negative thoughts toward ourselves or others create the inner disturbance that isolates us and sets us up for our drugs.
>
> **Lonely:** The "unconnected" sexaholic is a misconnection waiting to happen.
>
> **Tired:** Fatigue often seems to make us more liable to temptation, lowering our defenses somehow, as though becoming weak physically affects our emotional stamina.[1]
>
> ---
> 1: *Sexaholics Anonymous White Book, (1989) p. 34*

Just as an alcoholic can never consider himself to be cured, those who are addicted to pornography are always susceptible to relapse and should take proactive measures to stay in recovery for the rest of their lives. With time, remaining in recovery becomes easier.

The following factors can be used to help measure an addict's recovery:[9]

9: *For more information, see the chart in the* Handout *section of this manual, "Am I Serious About Dealing with My Pornography Problem?"*

- Is he completely honest, open, and transparent in discussing his pornography problem—past and present—with his spouse, parents, leaders, or loved ones?

- What has he done to facilitate his recovery? Did he fully disclose his problem, work the 12-Step program, and get counseling?

- Does he acknowledge himself as an addict and continue to attend 12-Step meetings and work with a sponsor to maintain recovery?

- How long has he gone without viewing pornography? Days? Months? Years?

- Is he learning to deal with life in a more constructive manner?

Finding a Qualified Counselor

Look for a therapist who has experience specifically treating sexual addiction. Sex and pornography addictions require therapists with special training. The following are general questions to consider when seeking a qualified sexual addiction therapist.

- **1. Q: What do you believe are the main adverse effects of the use of pornography?**
  A: Pornography use is destructive to the individual and makes healthy relationships impossible.

- **2. Q: Do you believe that pornography use can be classified as an addiction?**
  A: Yes. Current research demonstrates that the measurable changes in the brain caused by pornography viewing are very similar to the changes in the brain caused by addictive drugs and alcohol.

- **3. Q: Do you believe that recovery is possible?**
  A: Yes. It takes time and, like recovery from other addictions, there is no 'cure,' only long term sobriety and recovery.

- **4. Q: What is sobriety and what is recovery?**
  A: Sobriety is not having sex with self or others, other than your spouse. Recovery involves:

  - 1. *Come Out of Hiding.* Given the nature of addiction, it will be impossible to actually quit the behavior without the assistance of others. In secrecy, you may think you can overcome the addiction by willpower alone and may go for extended periods of abstinence. At some point, however, when the stress is right, isolation returns, and old patterns are rekindled and acting out in the addiction is inevitable.

  - 2. *Safe Environment.* Recovery is a lifestyle change. Activities, relationships or environments that expose a person seeking recovery to "triggering" circumstances greatly increase the chances for "slips" and relapse. Every effort must be made to "stay safe" by avoiding entertainment with sexual content as well as all known sexually triggering environments.

  - 3. *Education.* "The great aim of education is not knowledge but action."
    —Herbert Spencer

    "We give them a lot of reading to do in the sex addiction area…filled with successful recovery biographies.… We want them to be "world experts" on the nature of sex addiction, its genesis, its course, and helpful treatment procedures."
    —Dr. Victor Cline

  - 4. *Counseling.* "Sex and porn addictions require therapists with special training in these areas for patients to have a good chance of recovery. Anyone now seeking professional help will need to check very carefully the background experience of any therapists that they might chose to treat them. What you are looking for is a "sex addiction therapist" from any of the mental

health healing disciplines, who has a good track record in treating this problem and personal values that are reasonably congruent with the patient's values."

—Dr. Victor Cline

5. *Involve ecclesiastical leader(s).* "By this shall ye know if a man repenteth of his sins; behold, he will confess them and forsake them."

—Doctrine and Covenants 58:43

"Confession is a prerequisite to forsaking and helps others know of their sincere repentance."

—*He Restoreth My Soul*
by Donald L. Hilton Jr., MD

6. *Take refuge in God.* "We admitted we were powerless over lust, and our lives had become unmanageable."

—(Step 1 in the 12-Step program)

"Made a decision to turn our will and our lives over to the care of God as we understood Him."

—(Step 3 in the 12-Step program)

"Step Three calls for affirmative action for it is only by action that we can cut away the self-will which has always blocked the entry of God…into our lives."

—*White Book, Sexaholics Anonymous*

7. *Participating in 12 Step.* "Rarely have we seen a person fail who has thoroughly followed our path."

—*White Book, Sexaholics Anonymous*

"No one seems able to stay sober and progress in recovery without participating in the fellowship of recovery."

—*White Book, Sexaholics Anonymous*

Section 2

The 12 Step Program

Committing to participate in a 12-Step program is a critical element of the recovery process. It is usually when addicts finally admit that they are powerless to change on their own and become willing to join a 12-Step program that they find real recovery. 12-Step programs are non-professional, non-profit groups. Programs provide the following:

- Specific boundaries and recovery plans.

- Accountability to a sponsor and regular reporting at group meetings.

- Support and encouragement from others who are seeking recovery from addiction.

- A step-by-step process for pursuing recovery and making life changes.

- An emphasis on the need to turn to a Higher Power for help and intervention.

The "12 Steps of Recovery" *(see pages 48-49)* sets forth the steps individuals must follow to make the spiritual and mental changes that enable them to find and maintain long-term recovery. The steps were originally written and experienced by members of Alcoholics Anonymous. They closely correlate to the LDS view of the repentance process.

Productive participation in a 12-Step group initially requires attending several meetings per week, working the steps daily, and regularly reporting to a sponsor. A sponsor is someone who is working the 12-Steps, is in

strong recovery, and is willing to serve as a mentor. Their experience uniquely qualifies them to help others suffering from the same addiction. They promote accountability, give hope, and offer specific guidance on how to avoid relapses.

The LDS Church has two specific types of 12-Step groups. Addiction Recovery Program (ARP) meetings are open to men and women who want to recover from any type of addictive behavior. Pornography Addiction Support Group (PASG) meetings are for pornography addicts with a corresponding "Family Support Group" for spouses or loved ones.

There are also a number of non-LDS 12-Step groups that deal with sexual addiction. Sexaholics Anonymous (SA) groups are functioning in many areas and provide a very effective program for recovery from pornography and sexual addiction. S-Anon meetings are available to help those who are affected by someone else's sexual behavior, such as a spouse, parent, or other loved one.

Many of the benefits obtained from a 12-Step meeting come directly from the associations and interactions of the people who attend. Accordingly, the quality of 12-Step meetings can vary greatly. It is important to find a meeting that works for the person seeking recovery. Effective groups include the following:

- Regular meetings several times a week that are conducted by someone who is in recovery from the same addiction.

- Meetings with a reasonable number of people who have found healing and recovery and can share their experience, strength, and hope.

- Available sponsors who are qualified to guide newcomers through the recovery process.

- Literature specific to the addiction and a methodology for working the steps.

- A definition of sobriety that conforms to the value system of the individual seeking help.

If, after attending several meetings, the individual seeking help does not feel connected to the group, he may consider looking for a different 12-Step group. In areas where LDS PASG meetings are firmly established, church members have found great help and support. Many individuals have found that attending both PASG and SA/SAnon meetings can be helpful.

It is important to note that there are a number of non-LDS groups for sexual addiction. Sexaholics Anonymous has a definition of sexual sobriety consistent with LDS values: "No form of sex with one's self or with partners other than the spouse." Some of the other 12-Step programs for sexual addiction do not promote the same standard of sexual sobriety.

Discussing Pornography

PARENTS AND LEADERS *need to take an active role in ensuring that their family members and those within their stewardship have adequate, sound information to combat pornography. Because the topic can be a challenge, it is often avoided. Those within our stewardship, our ward members and family members, need to understand the physical, emotional, social, and spiritual damage caused by pornography.*

The information in this section provides suggestions that can be used to guide discussions and create lessons, and are intended to be used to promote discussion. (Sample lessons for different age groups may be found in Section 7.)

DISCUSSION POINTS FOR CHILDREN

The Importance of Our Bodies

- Our bodies are special gifts from our Father in Heaven. We need to value and take care of them, and show respect for this wonderful gift by dressing modestly.

- We each have a gender, boy or girl, and our gender is part of God's plan. Gender enables us to have children.

- Discuss what differentiates gender and how our bodies reproduce.

- As our bodies develop, we experience natural and good desires to reproduce.

- Explain the sacredness and joy of sex (reproduction) within the bounds of marriage.

Recognizing Pornography

- We are often tempted to act out natural sexual urges incorrectly, without any concern for what is good and right. Satan wants us to look at

pictures and videos of people who show their naked bodies and mock proper intimacy.

- Disrespect for our bodies can be shown in pictures, videos, and stories that can be found on TV and radio, and in books, movies, magazines, music, cell phones, iPods, video games, and websites. We call these kinds of inappropriate pictures, stories, and videos *pornography*.

How Pornography Can Hurt Us

- Looking at pornography can stop our ability to feel the Spirit.

- Pornography makes fun of our bodies and our sexuality, which are wonderful gifts from our Father in Heaven.

- Pornography tells lies about how people should treat each other.

- Once you start looking at pornography, it may become difficult to stop, even if you want to. Pornography creates incorrect beliefs and feelings about sexual intimacy, our bodies, and our eventual wife or husband. It can hurt the relationships we may have in our marriages some day.

- Pornography can hurt our ability to love and care about other people.

Avoiding Pornography

- If you ever see or hear anything that might be pornography, get away from it and talk to your parents. Do not be ashamed—your parents will be happy you told them, and it will feel right to talk about it. Seeing pornography should never be kept a secret.

- If a friend shows or talks about something that you think is pornography, tell him you don't want to see it and then leave. Make sure to talk to your parents about what happened.

- Only visit places on the Internet that your parents say are okay, and use the Internet when you are with adults. If you want to visit a site that you are not sure is okay to visit, ask your parents. If something comes up on your computer that you think is pornography, talk to your parents about it. *(For additional help and information, see the* Resource *section of this manual.)*

DISCUSSION POINTS FOR TEENS

What Is Pornography?

- Pornography is sexually explicit material that is intended primarily for sexual arousal.

- Pornography may include pictures in books, magazines, video games, and images on the Internet or your phone. It may also include lyrics in songs, movies, and inappropriate conversations.

Why Is Pornography Bad?

- Pornography is addictive. Extended use of pornography causes physical changes in the brain that make it very difficult to stop viewing by making the willpower center of the brain weak and the impulsive center of the brain strong.

- Viewing pornography is spiritually damaging and interferes with our ability to emotionally connect with family, friends, and God. It also severely damages us emotionally, physically, and socially.

- Pornography addiction often leads to improper sexual behavior with oneself or others.

- Pornography impairs our judgment: The desire for the next "fix" can cause us to make poor decisions we would not otherwise make.

- Pornography has a tendency to cause users to try to minimize, lie about, or keep their actions secret, thus undermining their integrity. They end up living "double lives."

- Pornography can cause us to develop unhealthy views of others and teaches lies about human sexuality. This can lead to sexual dysfunction and frustration in our intimate relationships in marriage.

◈ Pornography addiction can impede our ability to succeed in life and jeopardize our career.

◈ Viewing pornography usually escalates to other deviant sexual behavior.

Prevention

◈ A common lie is, "Just once won't hurt." Viewing pornography always hurts.

◈ When you see pornography, protect yourself by (1) thinking, "I should not look at pornography," (2) immediately turning off the program, video, or monitor, (3) doing another activity to get your mind off the pornography, and (4) talking with your parents.

◈ Avoiding pornography is difficult, but addiction is preventable. Talk to your parents if you are exposed, and avoid situations where exposure could happen.

◈ Consider the types of media you view and set definite standards. Install Internet filters and monitoring software on electronic devices, and learn Internet safety.

◈ Learn healthy sexuality by talking with parents and Church leaders. Talk to your parents about sexual development, so you can understand the truth when you are experiencing puberty. There is no question to be embarrassed about. Parents

are there to help you with any questions you may have.

What If I Keep Viewing Pornography?

◈ When you stop viewing pornography, then start again, stop again, and start again, it is likely that you are addicted.

◈ Recognize that recovering from a pornography addiction is possible, but difficult.

◈ Stop keeping your behavior a secret! Don't rationalize about whether or not you are "addicted" to pornography. If you have looked at pornography, discuss your behavior honestly with your bishop and parents. Get help so that you can experience recovery rather than just practicing white knuckle abstinence. In addition, it is important to recognize the power of the Atonement of Jesus Christ. Learn about and accept the Atonement of Jesus Christ, which is more powerful than your weakness.

◈ For more information and help, read:

 ◈ *A Parent's Guide* (www.lds.org)

 ◈ *Growing Up: Gospel Answers About Maturation and Sex* (Brad Wilcox)

DISCUSSION POINTS FOR YOUNG SINGLE ADULTS

What Is Pornography and Why Is It Bad?

◈ Pornography is sexually explicit material intended primarily for sexual arousal.

◈ Besides Internet exposure, pornography may be found in graphic romance novels and comic books, photographs, movies, images, games, erotic phone calls, and music.

◈ Pornography conditions us to develop totally one-sided, self-centered relationships, impeding our ability to connect emotionally and intimately with others. Romantic relationships and friendships are negatively affected. Pornography can lead to subsequent sexual dysfunction and frustration in our marriage relationships by establishing poor expectations and inappropriate sexual habits.

- Like drugs, pornography is extremely addictive. Viewing pornography causes physical changes in the brain which lead to addiction.

- Viewing pornography usually escalates to other deviant sexual behaviors.

- Pornography decreases our sensitivity to the Spirit, damaging our relationship with God.

- Pornography has caused many individuals to lose their jobs and suffer financial loss.

Prevention

- Choose movies and media carefully. Set standards and be accountable to the Lord.

- Practice Internet safety by installing filters and monitoring software and by placing computers in a public place.

- Anytime you feel enticed to look at pornography, discuss it with a trusted church leader. Acknowledge accidental exposures and what you can do to limit exposure in the future.

- Don't keep pornography viewing a secret; this feeds the addiction. Seek help—counsel with your bishop, honestly confess, and attend a 12-Step recovery group.

Dating and Pornography

- Openly discuss pornography early on in relationships so you can establish healthy communication patterns and not be blindsided by a hidden pornography habit.

- If you have struggled with pornography, it is important to tell the person you are dating the

nature and extent of the problem early on in the dating relationship.

- Be sensitive and respectful while asking, listening, or responding to another person's experience with pornography.

- Research has shown that it can take at least seven to twelve months of counseling, reporting to a bishop, and attending a 12-Step group before an addict significantly recovers. Even then it can take two to five years to achieve full recovery.

- Marriage will not fix a pornography problem. Even after marriage, a pornography problem is not overcome without help.

- Remember that the Atonement has real power and individuals can recover. Nevertheless, do not underestimate the power of pornography. Follow the Spirit in relationship decisions.

Recognizing and Overcoming a Pornography Problem

- If you keep telling yourself not to look at pornography but find yourself doing it anyway, you have a problem and it is very likely that you are addicted. Don't minimize the situation. Be completely honest and get help. Start by discussing your addiction problem with your bishop and parents.

◆ Know that the Atonement is real and that you can recover. Christ has the power to heal you, even though the physical chains of pornography addiction are strong.

◆ Learn about addiction and the recovery process: set boundaries, find a good therapist, and attend a 12 Step sexual addiction support group. Many have reported that participating in a 12-Step program was crucial for their recovery. 12-Step programs provide a sponsor, support group, and daily recovery program.

◆ For more information and help, read:

  ◆ *A Parent's Guide* (www.lds.org)

  ◆ *Growing Up: Gospel Answers About Maturation and Sex* (Brad Wilcox)

DISCUSSION POINTS FOR ADULTS

What Is Pornography and Why Is It Bad?

◆ Pornography is sexually explicit material intended primarily for sexual arousal.

◆ Besides Internet exposure, pornography may be found in graphic romance novels and comic books, photographs, movies, images, games, erotic phone calls, and music.

◆ Pornography conditions us to develop totally one-sided, self-centered relationships, impeding our ability to connect emotionally and intimately with others. Romantic relationships and friendships are negatively affected. Pornography can lead to subsequent sexual dysfunction and frustration in our marriage relationships by establishing poor expectations and inappropriate sexual habits.

◆ Like drugs, pornography is extremely addictive. Viewing pornography causes physical changes in the brain which lead to addiction.

◆ Viewing pornography usually escalates to other deviant sexual behaviors.

◆ Pornography decreases our sensitivity to the Spirit, damaging our relationship with God.

◆ Pornography has caused many individuals to lose their jobs and suffer financial loss.

Prevention

◆ Regularly discuss with your spouse (or adult confidant) the main gateways through which you (and your family members) are exposed to pornography. Identify means by which you can limit such exposure in the future.

◆ Set standards for yourself and your family regarding personal modesty and media consumption. Install effective filtering and monitoring software on electronic devices.

Recognition

◆ Lust is fundamental to sexual addiction. Lust is an attitude that is unnatural.

◆ Confront the issue if you think your spouse (or dating partner) has a problem. Respond to denial or defensiveness with a calm, determined attitude.

◆ It is a serious red flag if you are doing things which you wouldn't want your bishop, spouse, or close friends to know.

◆ If you keep telling yourself not to look at pornography and find yourself viewing it anyway, you have a problem. Don't minimize the situation: get help!

Recovery and Healing

◆ Replace fear with faith. There is hope for recovery, but it is important to get help.

- The elements of recovery for those addicted are:

  - Disclose the problem to your Church leader and, if applicable, your spouse.

  - Become educated regarding pornography addiction and the recovery process.

  - Find a qualified therapist (typically a minimum of 12 months of treatment is required).

  - Actively participate in a 12-Step program (get a sponsor, attend meetings, and work the program daily).

  - Install filtering, monitoring, and accountability programs on electronic devices. Set boundaries that minimize opportunities to consume pornography.

- The elements of healing for spouses, parents, and loved ones of addicts are:

  - Get support by speaking with ecclesiastical leaders, friends, and family.

  - Become educated, realize the other person's addiction is not your fault, break cycles of codependency, and let go of trying to control the other person.

  - Find a qualified therapist.

  - Find a sponsor who can help you set boundaries to protect yourself and the relationship. Attend a 12-Step program where you can get help and support from others who have experienced the same problems.

  - Slow down and take care of your personal needs.

- *Abstinence* from pornography is not *recovery*. Recovery requires lifestyle changes.

- In marriage, each spouse must be working on recovery before the relationship can heal.

- Allow time (usually at least one year) before making any permanent decisions regarding the marriage, for each spouse to heal.

- Healing is a spiritual process. Believe that through the Atonement you and your loved one can be made whole.

- Seek God's help in managing your life. Learn ways to manage life's natural challenges more successfully.

- Trust that you will find deep peace and joy when sexuality is exercised within the bounds the Lord has set.

- See the *Resource* section of this manual for more information and help.

FAQ

Frequently Asked Questions

QUESTIONS

General Information

Q 1 What is pornography?

Q 2 How is viewing pornography progressively addictive?

Q 3 What are the specifics of pornography and sexual addiction?

Q 4 How big of a problem is pornography?

Q 5 Is pornography a problem for women?

Q 6 If the problem is so big, why am I not more aware of it?

Q 7 Will discussing pornography make the problem worse or even raise curiosity?

Q 8 Why is pornography so dangerous?

Q 9 Is pornography addictive?

Q 10 What is sexual addiction?

Q 11 In what ways is pornography used as a "drug" or coping mechanism for other problems or kinds of stress?

Q 12 How can I tell if someone I love is addicted to pornography?

Q 13 What does "sobriety" mean?

Q 14 What does "recovery" mean?

Q 15 How does viewing pornography affect the friends of those who are addicted?

Q 16 How can I best support a recovering loved one?

Q 17 How can I best support a friend or loved one who is in a relationship with a pornography addict?

Q 18 What if a friend or loved one does not want recovery?

Q 19 What if my friend or loved one says he wants to recover, but continues to have relapses?

The 12-Step Program

Q 20 Why is attending a 12-Step meeting so important to recovery?

Q 21 What are 12-Step programs?

Q 22 What are the elements of a good 12-Step program?

Frequently Asked Questions

Q 23 What are the LDS based, ARP, PASG, and Family Support Group meetings?

Q 24 What are SA and S-Anon?

Q 25 What are the 12 Steps of recovery?

Q 26 What can I expect when I attend a 12-Step meeting?

Q 27 What does involvement in a 12-Step program entail?

Q 28 What is a sponsor?

Q 29 How can I find a good sponsor?

Q 30 Which is more important: a 12-Step support group or professional therapy?

Q 31 What if there is not a good 12-Step group in my area?

Q 32 What if the addict is a youth who is too young to attend 12-Step meetings?

Protecting Against Pornography

Q 33 How can I avoid pornography?

Q 34 How can I protect my child from pornography?

Q 35 What can I do in my home to increase Internet safety?

Q 36 As a parent, why should I be the one to teach my children about healthy sexuality?

Q 37 As a parent, when should I begin teaching about pornography and sexuality?

Q 38 How can I talk to my child about pornography and healthy sexuality?

Q 39 How should I respond if I discover my child is viewing pornography?

Do I Have a Problem?

Q 40 How can I tell if I have a pornography problem?

Q 41 Why is it important to be open and disclose my pornography problem to someone?

Q 42 Is recovery possible, and what does it involve?

Q 43 What recovery programs and resources are available for me as an addict?

Q 44 How do I find the right counselor?

Q 45 How do I "stay clean" or avoid relapse?

Q 46 How does viewing pornography affect me and my relationships?

Q 47 How does my viewing pornography affect my spouse or loved one?

Q 48 How does my viewing pornography affect my children?

Q 49 Does discovering or disclosing a pornography addiction generally result in divorce?

Q 50 As a recovering addict, what can I do to heal and strengthen my marriage?

Section 4

Spouses of Pornography Addicts

Q **51** How should I respond if I discover my spouse has a problem with pornography?

Q **52** Why can't my spouse just stop viewing pornography?

Q **53** How is the pornography addiction of a spouse or loved one likely to affect me personally?

Q **54** How is the pornography addiction of a spouse likely to affect our relationship?

Q **55** As the spouse of a pornography addict, what can I do to find healing for my damaged relationship?

Q **56** How do I find hope and healing for myself as the spouse of a pornography addict?

Q **57** What programs and resources are available for me as the spouse of a pornography addict?

Q **58** How do I balance my need for support and healing with my desire to maintain my spouse's anonymity?

Dating and Pornography

Q **59** Why should I discuss pornography with the person I am dating?

Q **60** When should I discuss pornography with the person I am dating?

Q **61** How should I discuss pornography with the person I am dating?

Q **62** What should I do if I suspect someone I am dating has a pornography problem?

Q **63** How is dating someone with a pornography addiction likely to affect me?

Q **64** What will likely happen if I choose to marry someone with a pornography addiction?

Q **65** As a recovering pornography addict, what factors should I consider in dating?

Q **66** What factors should I consider when deciding whether to continue a relationship with someone who is addicted to, has been addicted to, or is recovering from a pornography addiction?

Q **67** I am dating (or have dated) someone with a pornography problem and I am currently struggling with negative thoughts about myself and my appearance. What should I do?

Leaders

Q **68** How can I educate those I lead about the dangers of pornography?

Q **69** As a leader, how can I best help an individual with a pornography addiction?

Q **70** As a leader, how can I best help the spouse of an individual with a pornography addiction?

Q **71** What is an enabler?

Q **72** How can leaders, spouses, and parents avoid becoming enablers to those dealing with pornography and sexual addiction?

Q **73** What has a prophet and an apostle recently said to the brethren of the church about the seriousness of the plague of pornography?

ANSWERS

General Information

Q *1* **What is pornography?**

A **1** Pornography is "material that is sexually explicit and intended primarily for the purpose of

Section

4

sexual arousal."[1] It may depict nudity or sexual behavior, and includes written materials such as romance novels, photographs, movies, electronic images, video games, Internet chat rooms, erotic telephone conversations, music, or other media.[2]

Q 2   How is viewing pornography progressively addictive?

A 2   Dr. Victor Cline has explained the addictive process as follows: "In my experience as a sexual therapist, any individual who regularly masturbates to pornography is at risk of becoming, in time, a sexual addict, as well as conditioning himself into having a sexual deviancy and/or disturbing a bonded relationship with a spouse or girlfriend.

"A frequent side effect is that it also dramatically reduces their capacity to love (e.g., it results in a marked disassociation of sex from friendship, affection, caring, and other normal healthy emotions and traits which help marital relationships). Their sexual side becomes in a sense dehumanized. Many of them develop an "alien ego state" (or dark side), whose core is antisocial lust devoid of most values. In time, the "high" obtained from masturbating to pornography becomes more important than real life relationships. It makes no difference if one is an eminent physician, attorney, minister, athlete, corporate executive, college president, unskilled laborer, or an average 15-year-old boy. All can be conditioned into deviancy. The process of masturbatory conditioning is inexorable and does not spontaneously remiss. The course of this illness may be slow and is nearly always hidden from view. It is usually a secret part of the man's life, and like a cancer, it keeps growing and spreading. It rarely ever reverses itself, and it is also very difficult to treat and heal. Denial on the part of the male addict and refusal to confront the problem are typical and predictable, and this almost always leads to marital or couple

disharmony, sometimes divorce and sometimes the breaking up of other intimate relationships."[3]

Dr. Cline has summarized the progression as follows:

1. *Addiction*. The person finds he compulsively views pornography.

2. *Escalation*. The addicted person seeks progressively harder core pornography to get the same effect.

3. *Desensitization*. Tolerance increases to progressively explicit material.

4. *Acting Out Sexually*. The person seeks to act out fantasies viewed in the pornography (prostitution, adultery, etc.).[4]

Q 3   What are the specifics of pornography and sexual addiction?

A 3   Discussing the specifics of pornography can be uncomfortable. However, it is important that priesthood leaders, parents, and spouses understand in general terms the varying levels of pornographic material and associated experiences so they know what specific questions to ask and what to be aware of. Soft-core pornography generally consists of models posing topless or nude, as is common in *Playboy* magazines. Hardcore porn involves images of people actually engaging in graphic sexual acts or poses. On-demand pornography is available on the Internet for a cost, allowing viewers to specify the exact acts they want to see performed in front of the camera.

The sexual activity available at strip clubs varies greatly depending on state laws and the level of enforcement. At strip clubs, so-called lap dancing and other such activities may involve direct physical contact with private parts of the body. Some strip clubs have private rooms where simulation sex acts take place. As the sexual addiction progresses and

---

1: *Jill C. Manning, PhD, The Impact of Internet Pornography on Marriage and the Family: A Review of the Research, August 2005, Washington, D.C.*
2: *Jill C. Manning, PhD, What's the Big Deal About Pornography?, p 2–4.*

3: *Victor B. Cline, Pornography's Effects on Adult and Child, http://mentalhealthlibrary.info/library/porn/pornlds/pornldsauthor/links/victorcline/porneffect.htm.*
4: *Victor B. Cline, Pornography Effects on Adults and Children. Morality in Media, http://mentalhealthlibrary.info/library/porn/pornlds/pornldsauthor/links/victorcline/porneffect.htm.*

Section 4

escalates, addicts frequently become involved in activity with prostitutes and in other immoral, unbounded sexual encounters such as anonymous sex and one-night stands. The addicts' actions may eventually evolve into more deviant forms of sexual behavior, such as the viewing of child pornography, sexual abuse of self or others, rape, and sex in the context of violence.

Q 4 How big of a problem is pornography?

A 4 The following statistics are from various studies regarding pornography. Although more accurate information is needed, the following reflects the magnitude of the problem.

- Revenues from pornography now exceed the combined revenues of all professional football, baseball, and basketball franchises.[5]

- Some 34 million unique users (23% of all Internet users) visit pornography websites and view an average of 239 pornographic web pages each day.[6]

- Some 83% of youth watch pornography at home.[7]

- Of all consumers of online pornography, 72% are male and 28% are female.[8]

- Nearly 9 out of 10 (87%) young men and nearly one third (31%) of young women report viewing pornography.[9]

- 70% of men between the ages of 18 and 34 visit porn sites in a typical month.[10]

5: *"Internet Pornography Statistics." Internet Filter Review. Retrieved May 24, 2005, from http://internet-filterreview.toptenreviews.com/internet-pornography-statistics.html.*

6: *Nielsen//NetRatings, April 2005. Retrieved directly from Nielsen//NetRatings May 25, 2005.*

7: *E. Häggström-Nordin, U. Hanson, & T. Tydén, (2005). "Associations between Pornography Consumption and Sexual Practices among Adolescents in Sweden." International Journal of STD & AIDS, 16(2), 102–7.*

8: *Nielsen//NetRatings, April 2005. Retrieved directly from Nielsen//NetRatings May 25, 2005.*

9: *Generation XXX: Pornography Acceptance and Use Among Emerging Adults*

10: *Ibid.*

- The estimated age at which a child first sees online pornography is 11.[11]

- 47% of families in the United States say pornography is a problem in their home.[12]

- 9 out of 10 children between the ages of 8 and 16 have viewed pornography on the Internet, in most cases unintentionally.[13]

Q 5 Is pornography a problem for women?

A 5 While pornography use is currently not as common among women as it is for men, the number of women who view pornography is rapidly increasing. Seventy percent of new pornography websites are geared towards women. Pornography addiction in women frequently takes different forms than for men. For example, men tend to respond to visual images, while women initially tend to be more drawn to verbal and written forms of pornography such as graphic romance novels, explicit chat rooms, or online romantic role playing. Many women are drawn into social media relationships that can lead to the production of self-pornography for dissemination to individuals they meet online. Some women agree to watch pornography with their boyfriend or husband as a way to "spice up" the relationship or in an

11: *http://www.healthymind.com/s-porn-stats.html*

12: *http://www.safefamilies.org/sfStats.php*

13: *http://www.safefamilies.org/sfStats.php.*

Section

4

ineffective attempt to keep him from viewing it alone. In many cases, women can become addicted to the pornographic material. The same dangers of addiction and the same process of recovery that apply to men also apply to women.

Q 6   If the problem is so big, why am I not more aware of it?

A 6   Traditionally, the topic of pornography and sexual addiction has been taboo, so it was rarely discussed openly. There has been a stigma associated with the viewing of pornography along with an assumption that good people do not view it. This created a social culture that strongly resisted the recognition of pornography as a problem or addiction. Today, pornography is being marketed as a healthy pastime. Additionally, the idea is being perpetuated that only religious prudes with over-active guilt complexes disapprove of it. Much of society does not recognize pornography as a social concern. Unlike other addictions, pornography and sexual addiction are relatively easy to hide. This perpetuates the myth that pornography really is not a widespread problem. In actuality, it is a very widespread problem that needs to be discussed and addressed openly.

Q 7   Will discussing pornography make the problem worse or raise curiosity?

A 7   In society today, pornography is rampant; virtually all children will be exposed to pornography by the time they graduate from high school. As a result, it is necessary to discuss pornography openly. Without this discussion, children and teens are left with the impression that pornography is rather harmless. They are left totally unaware of its addictive nature and of the fact that regularly viewing pornography can destroy their ability to experience healthy and empathic relationships with others. Openness does not mean condoning immoral behavior or lessening consequences; instead, it involves teaching the truths about the consequences of viewing

pornography and creating a relationship where exposure to pornography is discussed.

Q 8   Why is pornography so dangerous?

A 8   While some people feel there is nothing wrong with pornography, evidence shows that there can be very real and dangerous effects on both individuals and society as a whole. Research indicates that pornography can be extremely addictive.[14] Pornography conditions a person to respond emotionally and sexually to a self-centered, artificial world.[15] Online chatrooms and romantic role playing, as well as pornography are not based in reality: what individuals "read and see about people, relationships, and sex is distorted."[16]

Research demonstrates that repeated exposure to pornography results in (1) increased callousness toward women, (2) trivialization of rape as a criminal offense, (3) distorted perceptions about sexuality, (4) increased appetite for more deviant and bizarre types of pornography, (5) devaluation of monogamy, (6) decreased satisfaction with a partner's sexual performance, affection, and physical appearance, (7) doubts about the value of marriage, (8) decreased desire to have children, and (9) viewing non-

14: http://www.surgicalneurologyint.com/browse.asp?sabs=n
15: Freeman-Longo, R. E. (2000). Children, Teens, and Sex on the Internet. Sexual Addiction & Compulsivity, 7, 75–90.
16: Ibid.

monogamous relations as normal and natural behavior.[17]

Q 9   Is pornography addictive?

A 9   Many wonder why those viewing pornography do not just stop when they have a sincere desire to do so, especially as they experience dramatic negative consequences associated with the behavior.

Most accept the concept that drugs and other substances can be addictive in a neurobiologic sense, in other words, they can change the chemistry and function of the pleasure/control centers of the brain, a process called neuromodulation. Can this happen with "natural" addictions also, such as with food, pathological gambling, and sexual addictions? The last ten years has produced research into the neurobiology of addiction which has provided strong evidence that the same "molecular switches" that induce and perpetuate drug addiction are also operative in natural addictions as well. This evidence supports the model that all addiction is perpetuated by an imbalance in the dopaminergic reward systems of the brain, this being associated with pathologically functioning control/reward centers.

The human brain is programmed to incentivize behaviors that contribute to survival. The mesolimbic dopaminergic system rewards eating and sexuality with powerful pleasure incentives. Cocaine, opioids, alcohol, and other drugs subvert, or hijack, these pleasure systems, and cause the brain to think a drug high is necessary to survive. Evidence is now strong that natural rewards such as food and sex affect the reward systems in the same way drugs affect them, thus the current interest in 'natural addiction.' Addiction, whether to cocaine, food, or sex occurs when these activities cease to contribute to a state of homeostasis, and instead cause adverse consequences.

There are some professionals as well as those involved in the pornography industry that disagree with the research and suggest that pornography may become a compulsion but not an addiction. The pornography industry and its apologists want to minimize any research pointing to an addictive basis for this devastating social and individual emotional illness. Rather than consider what is now a growing and substantial body of research supporting the existence of natural addiction, they attack or ignore any such research or researcher, generally saying that sure, pornography can be a "problem" for some. They obtusely point out that since there is no specific study on pornography, nothing can be said with regard to pornography as an addiction. In so doing they ignore current research as they minimize and marginalize.

Q 10   What is sexual addiction?

A 10   Sexual addiction is best described as a progressive intimacy disorder characterized by compulsive sexual thoughts and acts. Like other addictions, its negative impact on the addict and on family members increases as the disorder progresses. Over time, the addict usually has to escalate the addictive behavior to achieve the same results.

For some sex addicts, behavior does not progress beyond compulsive masturbation or the extensive use of pornography or phone or computer sex services. For others, addiction can involve strip clubs, soliciting prostitutes, or illegal activities such as exhibitionism, voyeurism, obscene phone calls, child molestation, or rape.

The National Council on Sexual Addiction and Compulsivity has defined sexual addiction as "engaging in persistent and escalating patterns of sexual behavior acted out despite increasing negative consequences to self and others." In other words, a sex addict will continue to engage in certain sexual behaviors despite facing potential health risks, financial problems, shattered relationships, or even arrest.

17: R.E. Drake, (1994). *Potential Health Hazards of Pornography Consumption as Viewed by Psychiatric Nurses. Archives of Psychiatric Nursing, 8(2),* p 101–106; Zillman, D., & Bryant, J. (1982). "Pornography, Sexual Callousness, and the Trivialization of Rape." *Journal of Communication, 32(4),* p 10–21; Zillman, D., & Bryant, J. (1984). "Effects of Massive Exposure to Pornography." In N. M. Malamuth & E. Donnerstein (Eds.), "Pornography and Sexual Aggression" (p 115–138). Orlando, FL: Academic; Zillman, D., & Bryant, J. (1988, December). "Effects of Prolonged Consumption of Pornography on Family Values." *Journal of Family Issues, 9(4),* p 518–544. Itzin, C. (2002). "Pornography and the Construction of Misogyny." *The Journal of Sexual Aggression, 8(3),* p 4-42. Cited in The Impact of Internet Pornography on Marriage and the Family: A Review of the Research, August 2005, Washington, D.C.*

Lust is the force behind sexual addiction: our healthy sexual feelings or our normal human sex drive are taken over by lust. Lust is the opposite of human intimacy; it's a self-indulgent fantasy which separates the sex from emotional connection. It is always insatiably 'hungry' and the addict will risk family, job, and church to indulge in this hunger. As one addict stated, "Lust is the most important thing in my life, it takes priority over me." (White Book, Sexaholics Anonymous, p 42).

The White Book further defines lust as:

◇ Not being able to say "no"

◇ Constantly being in dangerous sexual situations, i.e., viewing pornography at work, etc.

◇ Looking at women as if sex-starved, all the time

◇ Erotic fantasies

◇ Use of erotic media

The scriptures speak clearly on this topic:

> And he that looketh upon a woman to lust after her shall deny the faith, and shall not have the Spirit; and if he repents not he shall be cast out.
> —D&C 42:23
>
> But I say unto you, That whosoever looketh on a woman to lust after her hath committed adultery with her already in his heart.
> —Matthew 5:28

pornography becomes a drug used to cope with life problems, just as alcohol or illicit drugs might be used.

Every person finds ways to deal with the stress, anxiety, fear, boredom, and insecurity in their life. An addict is a person who has used addictive activities or substances as a way to deal with these things. Because pornography is readily accessible and can serve as a way to cope with anxiety, fear, boredom, etc., it often is used. This use can easily escalate into addiction.

> The acronym *HALT* is a reminder of conditions that make us more susceptible to relapse:
>
> **Hungry:** With many of us, an agitated state of mind—haste, hurry, or "hyper," for example—seems at least as perilous as hunger. And hunger itself can lead to binge eating, as many of us so well know. Binging on food can trigger the sexual addiction.
>
> **Angry:** Anger, resentment, and negative thoughts toward ourselves or others create the inner disturbance that isolates us and sets us up for our drugs.
>
> **Lonely:** The "unconnected" sexaholic is a misconnection waiting to happen.
>
> **Tired:** Fatigue often seems to make us more liable to temptation, lowering our defenses somehow, as though becoming weak physically affects our emotional stamina.[1]
>
> _____
> 1: Sexaholics Anonymous White Book, (1989) p. 34

Q 11   In what ways is pornography used as a "drug" or coping mechanism for other problems or kinds of stress?

A 11 While many individuals initially seek pornography out of a desire for excitement, anticipation, and pleasure, pornography is also often used as a way to escape from or cope with feelings of anxiety, fear, anger, stress, frustration, boredom, restlessness, loneliness, and insecurity. In this way,

Q 12   How can I tell if someone I love is addicted to pornography?

A 12 If you are concerned that a loved one might be viewing pornography, the best course of action is to ask him or her directly. The following questions may also help identify if there is a problem. It is important to note that some of these conditions are common and may not necessarily be caused by pornography use, but by other life conditions or circumstances.

Physical Behaviors:

- Have you caught your loved one viewing inappropriate material or found pornographic material for which your loved one denies responsibility?

- Does your loved one spend time on the computer after everyone else is in bed or stay up late for unexplained reasons?

- Does your loved one quickly change the computer screen or turn off the computer when you walk by or enter the room?

- Does your loved one frequently clear the Internet history on the computer?

- Does your loved one have substantial amounts of unaccounted-for time and avoid disclosing his or her activities?

- Is your loved one working long hours at the office over prolonged periods of time for unexplained reasons?

- Does your loved one seem tired or worn out? When questioned, do his answers seem odd or unsatisfactory?

- Is your loved one missing appointments and deadlines without a satisfactory explanation?

- How does your loved one respond when you address the topic of pornography? Does he

initially seem uncomfortable, hostile, or non-responsive?

- Does your loved one seek out and view increasingly graphic and sexually explicit movies and TV shows?

Relational Behaviors:

- Does your loved one seem withdrawn, "checked out," or emotionally disconnected for long periods of time?

- Does your loved one spend less time with the family or seek isolation frequently?

- Does your loved one seem more irritable and on edge?

- Have you experienced a "gut feeling" that something is wrong?

- Does your loved one seem to be unable to see his or her part in relationship conflicts, and instead blames others when discussing such issues?

- Does your loved one become angry over little things?

- Do you periodically notice sharp contrasts in behavior which might include being more disconnected, uninvolved, and critical?

- Has your loved one become more concerned with or critical of physical appearances?

- Does your loved one send conflicting messages regarding his or her feelings and desires for your relationship?

Financial Behaviors:

- Are there charges on your credit card statements to unfamiliar companies?

- Are there long-distance phone charges to unknown numbers on your phone bill?

- Are there unaccounted-for expenditures?

Sexual Behaviors:

- ❖ Does your spouse seem to go unusually long periods of time between sexual intimacy?

- ❖ Does your spouse seem to pressure you for sex even when you make it clear that it is not something you want to do?

- ❖ Does your spouse seek to experiment with sexual behaviors that you find uncomfortable or unacceptable?

- ❖ Does your spouse ask you to view sexually explicit material to improve or "spice up" your sex life?

Q 13   What does sobriety mean?

A 13 Sexaholic Anonymous has defined sobriety as "having no form of sex with self or with persons other than the spouse."[18] In addition, true sexual sobriety "includes progressive victory over lust[,] ...the driving force behind sexual acting out."[19] According to the Sexaholics Anonymous *White Book*:

"Physical sobriety is not an end in itself but a means towards an end–victory over the obsession and progress in recovery…. In practical terms, we stop entertaining lustful fantasy. We stop using the Internet to look for pornography images…. We choose a different route to avoid places where lust triggered us or we acted out…. If we are going to a business or event where we know there will be lust or sexual triggers (such as a supermarket, mall, hotel, or an airport), we call someone…. If we are uncomfortable in any given situation, we simply leave…. Our sobriety becomes the most important thing each day in every circumstance."

Q 14   What does recovery mean?

A 14 Recovery from pornography or sexual addiction requires more than just stopping or abstaining from the behavior. Abstinence from viewing

18: *White Book. Sexaholics Anonymous, p 191–192.*
19: *Ibid.*

pornography is important, of course, but true recovery requires a lifestyle change and a change of heart. It includes recognizing and admitting to being an addict, setting appropriate boundaries to protect against future acting out, learning to cope with life's challenges in healthy and appropriate ways, being willing to work on recovery daily, and changing the underlying behaviors that cause the individual to seek out pornography. Some factors that can indicate a person's progress in recovery include:

- ❖ Is he completely honest, open, and transparent in discussing his pornography problem—past and present?

- ❖ What steps are being taken to recover?

  - ✦ Does he fully disclose his problem to his spouse, significant other, parents, therapist, and religious leaders?

  - ✦ Does he work with a sponsor?

  - ✦ Does he participate in a 12-Step program?

  - ✦ Is he getting appropriate counseling?

- ❖ Does he still acknowledge his addiction and continue working recovery?

- ❖ How long has he gone without viewing pornography? Research has shown that it takes at least seven to twelve months before an addicted individual is on his way to establishing true and lasting sobriety. Complete recovery requires time.

- ❖ Does the person work on issues underlying his pornography addiction? Is the person working to change attitudes and behaviors regarding healthy sexuality, developing relationship skills, learning to address unresolved problems, and dealing with life more constructively?

- ❖ Is he concerned about helping others who might also be suffering from pornography addiction more than keeping his experiences with pornography a secret?

Ⓠ 15 How does viewing pornography affect the friends of those addicted?

Ⓐ 15 Being addicted to pornography can also cause the individual to be emotionally unavailable, thus creating a distance in relationships. Discovering a pornography addiction may be especially devastating. Often friends of those addicted will initially experience feelings of disbelief, fear, disgust, betrayal, distrust, shock, denial, sadness, and anger. Individuals may wonder if they can ever trust the addict, if the addict poses a danger, and why the addict would continue in such behavior.

Some people may deal with these emotions by withdrawing from the relationship. Others may try to maintain a feeling of normalcy by avoiding the issue and pretending nothing has changed. Others may try to inappropriately step in and try to fix the problem without having the tools and skills necessary to help the individual truly recover. Friends of a pornography addict may experience a grieving process similar to what a spouse undergoes. It is important for them to identify and learn to work through these emotions.

Ⓠ 16 How can I best support a recovering loved one?

Ⓐ 16 One of the most painful parts of supporting a recovering addicted loved one is coming to accept the lack of control over whether the addict chooses to pursue recovery. Recovery is the addict's personal responsibility. Addicts have to become ready and willing to find recovery for themselves. It is often difficult for a spouse or friend to find the balance

between patience, encouragement, and acceptance versus enabling destructive behavior. Do not confuse attempts to micromanage the addict's recovery with true support and encouragement. A few important elements to keep in mind are:

- Focus on personal choices that you can make regardless of the other person's decisions. Take responsibility for your own peace and emotional well-being.

- Get help for yourself and recognize the ways that being in a close relationship with an addict will likely affect you. Many find counseling and a 12-Step program to be critical in this process.

- Do not take responsibility for the addict's recovery. Recognize and accept that being a "policeman" is not helpful to the addict. The addict must ultimately choose his own course of action.

- Set boundaries and have the commitment to stick to them. Although an addict makes his own choices, he cannot dictate the choices of others or avoid the consequences of violating the boundaries of others.

- Try to identify ways in which the addicted individual is reaching out for help and recovery. Find ways to connect with him that are emotionally supportive, safe, and uplifting. Reaching out can be a tremendous source of encouragement and support.

Ⓠ 17 How can I best support a friend or loved one who is in a relationship with a pornography addict?

Ⓐ 17 When individuals are in a relationship with a pornography addict, they frequently feel isolated, alone, or helpless. Friends or loved ones of those who are directly affected by the pornography addiction of another can best help by being available to support them. Listen and allow your friend to share his or her feelings in a safe, confidential environment. Do not

Section

4

tell that person that you know what it is like. Do not try to solve the individual's problems or tell her what should be done. Encourage the individual to seek appropriate professional and religious counseling, find a sponsor, and attend meetings of support groups. Let the suffering individuals know that they are loved, accepted, and supported as they make important decisions. Learn about pornography addiction, and encourage your friend to do the same.

18 What if a friend or loved one does not want recovery?

A 18 Ultimately, the person struggling with the pornography addiction must be the one to decide if he wants to do the work and make the lifestyle changes necessary for recovery. Continue to be understanding and supportive, but make sure you understand the problem of becoming codependent or enabling the addict in his or her behavior. Encourage the addict to get help. Regardless of whether an addict wants to recover, it is important to provide support to the spouse and other loved ones of the addict. Encourage them to get appropriate help and to set boundaries for protection in the relationship.

19 What if my friend or loved one says he wants to recover, but continues to have relapses?

A 19 Although a relapse can be a setback, what really matters most is the actions the addict chooses to take after a relapse. Does the individual try to excuse or minimize his return to pornography, or is

he contrite, and shows a broken heart? Help addicts understand that suffering a relapse does not mean they are a lost cause. Feelings of shame, humiliation, and worthlessness can compound addictive behavior. Assure the addict that God loves him and will help him gain recovery. At the same time, do not minimize or disregard inappropriate behavior. Help the addict realize that the relapse is serious. If appropriate, ask questions about what events may have triggered it. Encourage him to be regularly accountable to someone about his behavior choices, continue to attend 12-Step meetings, and work with a sponsor and therapist. Addicts can learn from their mistakes as they seek appropriate counsel and guidance.

Recovery is hard work and requires serious lifestyle changes. By encouraging the individual to identify specific steps to avoid future slips and by expressing love and support, you can help him find hope, determination, and the courage needed to continue in his recovery program.

The 12-Step Program

20 Why is attending a 12-Step meeting so important to recovery?

A 20 For those who are seeking recovery, committing to participate in a 12-Step program is often a critical milestone in the recovery process. Many people have attempted to stop viewing pornography on their own, only to eventually fail. For many addicts, it is only when they break the secrecy surrounding their addiction, admit that they will not be able to change on their own, and join a 12-Step fellowship that real recovery is found. The *White Book* of Sexaholics Anonymous states:

We sexaholics do not presume to be authorities on addiction of any kind, much less sex addiction…. Some researchers even confess to being baffled by what addiction really is…. We speak from our own experience as seen through recovery.[20]

20: Ibid. Pg. 29

We have a solution. We don't claim that it's for everybody, but for us, it works. There is an unwritten step underlying all twelve. Call it Step Zero: "We participated in the fellowship of the program."[21] No one seems able to stay sober and progress in recovery without it, though some try. For most of us, without associating in some way with other recovering individuals, there is no lasting sobriety and none of the fringe benefits of recovery, growth, freedom, and joy… We don't try to explain this; it is simply a fact [emphasis added]."[22]

For those closely influenced by the addiction of another, attending a 12-Step program is also important. One of the least understood components of sexual addiction is the devastating effect it can have on a spouse or loved one. In the process of trying to cope with the problems of living with a sex addict, a spouse or loved one frequently develops his or her own set of negative behaviors or codependent habits that are debilitating to the individual and destructive to relationships. Regardless of whether the addict chooses to follow a recovery program, the spouse or loved one of an addict should work out his or her own recovery. Attending 12-Step meetings is a vital part of that recovery.

It is important to note that support groups, or 12-Step programs, are not substitutes for therapeutic treatment; individuals should also seek appropriate professional counseling as a key part of their recovery process.

⒬ 21 What are 12-Step programs?

Ⓐ 21 12-Step programs have been unusually successful in helping those struggling with addiction find recovery. There are over 100 different variations of 12-Step recovery programs in existence today. They address virtually every imaginable type of addiction. All of them, including the LDS Addiction Recovery Program (ARP), are based on the original 12-Step program of Alcoholics Anonymous and the *AA Big Book* (first published in 1939). Other

21: *Ibid. Pg. 2*
22: *Ibid. Pg. 63*

12-Step programs deal with specific issues such as drug addiction, food addiction, codependency, over-spending, and gambling. 12-Step programs are non-professional and non-profit. While effective in promoting recovery from addiction, they are not intended to replace therapy led by trained professionals. All 12-Step programs share a number of elements that aid in the recovery process:

- ◆ **Openness:** Breaking the shame and secrecy surrounding an addiction is one of the first steps in overcoming it. Meetings provide a safe, supportive environment to share feelings and experiences with others who understand what you are going through because they have experienced the same thing.

- ◆ **Specific Boundaries and Recovery Plan:** A 12-Step program can provide specific rules and definitions of abstinence or sobriety that are used to measure progress and recovery. The program also offers literature and instructions for recovery that can be used daily to help individuals overcome addiction.

- ◆ **Accountability:** Addicts check in frequently with a sponsor and also report their progress at meetings. These interactions provide accountability and transparency. They also help to dissipate the shame surrounding addiction so the addict can focus on the actions needed to achieve recovery.

- ◆ **Support:** Recovering addicts share their experience, strength, and hope with new members who are just starting the recovery process. Newer and more experienced addicts in recovery all find support and encouragement by attending meetings, talking with other group members, making outreach calls, reading literature, working with a sponsor, or serving as a sponsor.

- ◆ **The 12 Steps:** Working the steps daily is critical to addressing the emotional and spiritual issues behind the addiction. Daily effort is necessary to achieve long-term success.

- *Higher Power:* All 12-Step programs focus on turning to a Higher Power for intervention and healing. Most 12-Step programs are non-denominational. They are careful to define the concept of God as broadly as possible so their program can feel inclusive to as many people as possible. Latter-day Saints who participate in 12-Step groups understand this Higher Power to be our Heavenly Father and recognize that recovery of both addicts and loved ones comes through the power of the Atonement of Jesus Christ.

- Watch the video by Dr. Patrick Carnes, "Why Are 12-Steps So Effective?" on the SA Lifeline Foundation website. (www.salifeline.org)

Q 22 What are elements of a good 12-Step program?

A 22 Much of the benefit obtained from attending a 12-Step meeting is derived from the other members present. Accordingly, the efficacy of 12-Step meetings is as varied as the people who attend them. It is important to find a meeting that works for the individual seeking help. Depending on the availability in the area, many LDS members in recovery have found both LDS-sponsored and non-LDS meetings to be extremely helpful. Effective groups will have:

- Meetings attended regularly by a reasonable number of people who have found healing and recovery and who can share their experience, strength, and hope.

- Available sponsors who are experienced and qualified to guide newcomers through the recovery process.

- Recommended literature specific to the addiction, and a methodology for working the 12 Steps.

- A definition of sobriety consistent with the value system of the individual seeking recovery.

- Regular meetings several times each week conducted by someone who has gained recovery from the specific addiction.

If, after attending several meetings of a particular 12-Step group, the individual seeking recovery does not have a positive experience, he should look for a different group that can better meet his needs and matches the above criteria. It is important to not give up until a group is found that works for the individual. See *www.salifeline.org* for more information on finding 12-Step meetings, both LDS-sponsored and non-LDS.

Q 23 What are the LDS based ARP, PASG, and Family Support Group meetings?

A 23 The LDS Church sponsors several 12-Step recovery groups. Addiction Recovery Program (ARP) meetings are open to men and women who want to recover from any type of addictive behavior, and they use the 12 Steps as a sequential way to better apply the Atonement of Jesus Christ. The Pornography Addiction Support Group (PASG) is specifically for pornography or sexual addiction, and the corresponding Family Support Group is for the loved ones of those addicted. The PASG and Family Support Group meetings follow the same format as ARP meetings and use the same manual, the *Addiction Recovery Program: A Guide to Addiction Recovery and Healing.* The LDS Family Service's program is also working on a family support guide to assist those who have a loved one in addiction.

The manual, as well as ARP, PASG, and Family Support Group meetings, can help individuals by continually reinforcing the connection between gospel principles, reliance on our Father in Heaven, and the Atonement of Jesus Christ in the recovery process. The number of people attending meetings and the frequency of meetings held can vary greatly depending on the location. If your area does not have a strong

PASG program, LDS members seeking recovery can help strengthen their local program by going to non-LDS groups to gain recovery and then return to share their experience with the LDS group.

24 What is SA and S-Anon?

A 24 Sexaholics Anonymous (SA) is a 12-Step program designed specifically for those who are struggling with sexual addiction, which includes pornography.[23] S-Anon is a 12-Step program designed to help those who are affected by someone else's addictive sexual behavior.[24] While these programs are non-denominational, their principles are very similar to those of the LDS faith. It is important to note that there are a number of other non-LDS groups for sexual addiction. An advantage of SA in particular is that its definition of sexual sobriety is consistent with LDS beliefs: "No form of sex with one's self or with partners other than the spouse [and] progressive victory over lust." Some other groups do not necessarily promote the same standards of chastity, but instead encourage members to create their own definition of "sobriety." As LDS members look for appropriate 12-Step groups, they should make sure that the group's definition of sobriety matches their belief system. Many members of the LDS faith have found SA and S-Anon, along with PASG, to be especially effective in helping them achieve recovery.

25 What are the 12 Steps of recovery?

A 25 The 12 Steps of recovery set forth the process by which individuals make spiritual, emotional, and mental changes that enable them to recover from addictive behavior and maintain long-term abstinence or sobriety. The steps were originally written and published by Alcoholics Anonymous, but very closely correlate to the process of repentance and applying the Atonement of Jesus Christ. An LDS version of the 12 Steps has been reworded slightly to more accurately reflect correct doctrine as taught in The Church of Jesus Christ of Latter-day Saints.

The original wording of each step as written by Alcoholics Anonymous is given on the following pages, in parenthesis are the two word changes made by Sexaholics Anonymous, followed by the LDS wording for that step.

23: See http://www.sa.org

24: See http://www.sanon.org

Section 4

The 12 Steps of Recovery

STEP 1

We admitted we were powerless over our addiction (lust)—that our lives had become unmanageable.

(Honesty) Admit that you, of yourself, are powerless to overcome your addictions and that your life has become unmanageable.

STEP 2

Came to believe that a Power greater than ourselves could restore us to sanity.

(Hope) Come to believe that the power of God can restore you to complete spiritual health.

STEP 3

Made a decision to turn our will and our lives over to the care of God as we understood Him.

(Trust in God) Decide to turn your will and your life over to the care of God the Eternal Father and His Son, Jesus Christ.

STEP 4

Made a searching and fearless moral inventory of ourselves.

(Truth) Make a searching and fearless written moral inventory of yourself.

STEP 5

Admitted to God, to ourselves, and to another human being the exact nature of our wrongs.

(Confession) Admit to yourself, to your Heavenly Father in the name of Jesus Christ, to proper priesthood authority, and to another person the exact nature of your wrongs.

STEP 6

Were entirely ready to have God remove all these defects of character.

(Change of Heart) Become entirely ready to have God remove all your character weaknesses.

STEP 7

Humbly asked God to remove our shortcomings.

(Humility) Humbly ask Heavenly Father to remove your shortcomings.

STEP 8

Made a list of all persons we had harmed, and became willing to make amends to them all.

(Seeking Forgiveness) Make a written list of all persons you have harmed and become willing to make restitution to them.

STEP 9

Made direct amends to such people wherever possible, except when to do so would injure them or others.

(Restitution and Reconciliation) Wherever possible, make direct restitution to all persons you have harmed.

STEP 10

Continued to take personal inventory and when we were wrong promptly admitted it.

(Daily Accountability) Continue to take personal inventory, and when you are wrong, promptly admit it.

STEP 11

Sought through prayer and meditation to improve our conscious contact with God as we understood Him, praying only for knowledge of God's will for us and the power to carry that out.

(Personal Revelation) Seek through prayer and meditation to know the Lord's will and to have the power to carry it out.

STEP 12

Having had a spiritual awakening as the result of these steps, we tried to carry this message to alcoholics (sexaholics) and to practice these principles in all our affairs.

Having had a spiritual awakening as a result of the Atonement of Jesus Christ, share this message with others and practice these principles in all you do.

Q 26   What can I expect when I attend a 12-Step meeting?

A 26   At 12-Step meetings, a group leader will generally begin by reading verbatim a set script, followed by readings from selected program literature and an opportunity for group members to share with others about the readings or their specific recovery experiences. As is tradition, speakers generally introduce themselves by first name only, after which the group responds, "Hi, _____ [name]." Although the format of the meetings may feel odd to newcomers, the script soon becomes familiar and comfortable as the attendees learn the importance of each concept. There are no dues or fees for membership, although a basket will generally be passed around at non-LDS meetings so that attendees can contribute a dollar or two in order to meet obligations of rent and operating costs.

Q 27   What does involvement in a 12-Step program entail?

A 27   Initially, involvement in a 12-Step program usually entails attending a minimum of three meetings per week. Some programs encourage even more.

Attending a meeting specifically designed for your addiction is ideal. However, it can still be useful to attend other types of 12-Step meetings, especially if meetings for your particular addiction are not available. If meetings are not readily available locally, an increasing number of live telephone or online meetings can also be found.

Working the 12 Steps daily is what makes the 12-Step program work. This process includes studying prescribed literature, journaling, and reporting on commitments made to a sponsor. Having a sponsor is critical to the recovery process. As progress in recovery is achieved, those in recovery have the opportunity to fill service positions within the program. This may include being a sponsor, being responsible for the group's literature library, acting as a secretary to the group, or serving as liaison to the 12-Step group's regional body. Maintaining recovery requires that we "give back what [we] have so generously been given."[25] Many recovery addicts report that the most effective way to safeguard their own sobriety and recovery is to work closely with other addicts who are also trying to recover.

25: "SA Script" (www.sa.org)

Section

4

Weak strands, woven together, create a nearly invincible rope.

Q 28 What is a sponsor?

A 28 Sponsorship is a critical component of all 12-Step programs. Sponsors are those who are working the 12 Steps and have found sobriety and recovery from a specific addiction. Because of their experience, they are in a unique position to help guide others suffering from the same addiction through the recovery process. They provide hope, accountability, and specific guidance on how to avoid relapse. The literature of one 12-Step program encourages the newcomer to "find a sponsor who has what you want and ask how it was obtained."[26] A sponsor will give assignments designed to help gain and maintain recovery. The assignments may include specific rules of conduct, attendance at meetings, reading various kinds of literature, and reporting on a designated schedule. Typically those struggling with addiction call their sponsor at set intervals to report their progress and get support or practical feedback as they encounter daily problems. The addicted individual may also call a sponsor or any other program member at any time when he feels tempted to act out.

While the need for addicts to have a sponsor is generally recognized, many people do not understand the critical role that a sponsor can play in the recovery of an addict's spouse or loved one. The spouse's sponsor can give support and validation and help the loved one understand that she is not responsible for the addict's behavior. The sponsor can also help the spouse or loved one set healthy boundaries for personal protection.

The LDS ARP program generally uses the term *support person*, acknowledging that recovery is facilitated by having a specific person from whom an addict can receive confidential advice, encouragement, and support.

Q 29 How can I find a good sponsor?

A 29 Sponsors can be found at 12-Step meetings. Although anyone who is in recovery from a specific addiction can generally be a sponsor, it is important to find a sponsor who will work well with the individual seeking help. It is also important to remember that each sponsor offers unique insights and perspectives. At different points in the recovery process, individuals may feel a need to change sponsors. Considerations in selecting a sponsor may include:

- Sponsors ordinarily should not be related or closely associated with the individual (i.e., a spouse, partner, family member, loved one, or even close friend). They need to provide an impartial perspective.

- Sponsors should be emotionally and spiritually stable in their own recovery. Unless they have thoroughly worked the steps and continue to do so, they cannot provide the insight necessary to help someone else.

- Sponsors should be readily available, be willing to accept phone calls, and encourage those they sponsor to reach out to them whenever needed.

- Sponsors should keep confidences and maintain the anonymity of the person they are helping.

- Most programs suggest that sponsors be of the same gender as the addict. This is especially important for pornography and sexual addiction.

- Sponsors should hold individuals to their commitments. A good sponsor is someone who is honest and corrects the addict when he starts minimizing commitments or slipping into addictive or enabling behaviors.

- Sponsors must care about the individual. Effective sponsors will listen with empathy and act out of love and a desire to help the individual they sponsor succeed.

Q 30 Which is more important: 12-Step support groups or professional therapy?

A 30 12-Step groups and professional counseling are equally important to recovery. Most individuals

---

26: Alcoholics Anonymous Big Book script

Click Here for Table of Contents

who successfully recover spend a substantial amount of time in both counseling and the 12-Step program. Even though 12-Step support will serve as the foundation for long-term recovery, professional treatment provides a critical component for individual and relationship healing. For most people, a multi-dimensional approach works best. Like constructing a strong rope, the real strength is not in the individual strands, but in weaving many strands together. A balanced recovery program will include an open-ended period of 12-Step support, individual and couples counseling, group counseling, education, proper nutrition and exercise, spirituality, and other lifestyle changes. Even though a handful of individuals and couples have apparently experienced recovery doing only one or the other, the majority of individuals and couples benefit from, and may even require, a multi-dimensional approach.

② 31 What if there is not a good 12-Step group in my area?

Ⓐ **31** It is important to be aware of how effective the 12-Step groups are in your area at helping individuals find recovery. For specific information on organizing SA meetings, visit *www.sa.org*. To organize S-Anon meetings, see *www.sanon.org*. To request that a LDS PASG or Family Support Group meeting be created in your area, contact your local LDS Family Services, *www.providentliving.org/ses/emotionalhealth/contact/1,12169,2128-1,00.html.*

② 32 What if the addict is a youth who is too young to attend 12-Step meetings?

Ⓐ **32** Many children and youth are now addicted to pornography. Without appropriate help, their addiction can inhibit their ability to form healthy, emotional relationships with anyone. Because of the special considerations for teens, there are no regular, public 12-Step meetings available. There are counselors who specialize in this age group. Additionally, some therapists offer group sessions specifically for youth.

Protecting Against Pornography

② 33 How can I avoid pornography?

Ⓐ **33** Because of the changes in the way information is disseminated through high-speed media, there is no way to completely avoid pornography. Accidental exposure occurs even with the best software filtering programs. There are, however, some ways to decrease exposure. The most important method is to be personally committed to self-regulation. Individuals must be ready to turn away from provocative images that are displayed in advertising, written material, magazines, movies, television, games, and any electronic device connected to the Internet. Decreasing exposure to media is a good way to reduce the desensitizing process that occurs in our hyper-sexualized culture. It's important to note that today's mainstream media contains sexualized content that would have been considered "soft-core" pornography 30 years ago.

As an individual, you must establish personal standards ahead of time to avoid offensive, immoral, or pornographic material. Not only is decreasing exposure to such media important, but it is also important to personally monitor ongoing emotional and relational health that could increase vulnerability.

Section

4

Q 34 How can I protect my child from pornography?

A 34 Education is essential in helping children become aware of the dangers involved with using pornography. Most people do not know that viewing pornography can quickly turn into a lifelong addiction that is extremely difficult to overcome. Teach children what to watch out for and how to respond when they encounter pornographic images or information. Regular, open communication about pornography with family members reinforces the commitment to core values and family rules that are established and agreed upon.

Vigilance is required even after taking precautions. Parents should be aware that the vast majority of pornography is viewed in the home—either their own home or that of a friend—so they need to establish rules regarding Internet use. Although filters will not prevent a child from viewing pornography if that child is determined to do so, it will provide an initial delay and block most easy or accidental access. Having discussions about media use, posting guidelines for computers, and drafting a family pledge signed by all members may be beneficial. Additionally, watching for negative changes in a child's behavior is important. If any such changes are noticed or a parent is concerned about possible pornography use, it is important to talk to the child and get help immediately if needed. (See Lesson Plans for additional teaching resources.)

External monitoring and internal monitoring are both needed to protect children from pornography. External monitoring has to do with identifying possible ways your child could be exposed to pornography and finding ways to decrease the chance of exposure. Internal monitoring teaches a child to recognize pornography, how to respond to it and helps them create an internal value system. Parents should have regular talks with their children about their sexuality, exposure to pornography, how to respond to this exposure, and the value of chastity and sexual restraint. Parents need to feel confident that when their child is accidentally exposed to pornography, the child knows how to respond to it and will tell their parents about it. This internal monitoring helps give the child tools he needs to courageously make the right choices.

Q 35 What can I do in my home to increase Internet safety?

A 35 Individuals and parents can do many things to safeguard their homes from the harmful influences found on the Internet. While there is no foolproof system, some simple steps can help reduce the risk of family members encountering pornographic materials. Please visit *www.salifeline.org* for more information.

- Become educated about computers and how the Internet works. Your Internet browser allows you to view a history of sites that have been visited (although the history can be deleted).

- Place computers in high-traffic areas of the home. Kitchens and family rooms usually have the most traffic. Because these rooms usually do not have doors, they are typically less secluded than bedrooms. Position computer monitors so the screen faces outward for public view.

- Install Internet filters on electronic devices. Learn their features and how to use them. Good filtering programs have an un-erasable history of websites (including chat rooms) that have been visited and when they were visited. They can also provide a record of incoming and outgoing emails. Some filters allow you to password-protect the Internet or certain types of websites. Others allow you to set limits on when the Internet is accessible.

- Teach family members about the dangers of Internet pornography, including how to escape if an inappropriate site is accidentally accessed. Usually it is recommended to just push the off button to shut down the entire system or to walk away.

- Teach children to tell their parents if they encounter any form of pornography while on the computer or elsewhere. This will help reduce the fear or shame of accidental exposure. It also serves to open discussion about the dangers of pornography.

◆ Teach family members to use the Internet for a specific purpose only. Aimless surfing makes it easier to happen to accidentally encounter inappropriate sites.

◆ Teach family members to avoid public and private chat rooms, bulletin boards, forums, or unfamiliar areas on the Internet. Such places present a substantial risk for children and adults.

◆ Teach children not to share any personal information online without parental knowledge and permission. Many predators pose as children to gain access to information that may put children at risk.

◆ Be aware of the policies of your children's school and the local public library regarding Internet use and accessibility.

◆ Teach family members to never open email from someone they don't know. Even emails apparently from those you know could be a problem.[27]

② 36 As a parent, should I be the one to teach my children about healthy sexuality?

Ⓐ 36 Our culture is filled with misleading and destructive messages about sexuality. If we let children learn about sexuality from the media and other influences that surround them, they are unlikely to develop a healthy concept of sex. When children understand healthy sexuality, they are better prepared to counter the unhealthy myths about sex and can better understand why pornography is so destructive. Parents must actively seek opportunities to teach children about gender roles, sex, and love. This should include the physical, emotional, and spiritual aspects of sex, including the proper, healthy role of sexual intamacy within a marriage relationship. Given the prevalence of sexual and pornographic material in the world, teaching should begin early if parents wish to be the principal shapers of their children's attitudes about sex. Teaching about healthy sexuality helps build openness, trust,

and love, which allow children to feel comfortable discussing other subjects with their parents as well.

② 37 As a parent, when should I begin teaching about pornography and sexuality?

Ⓐ 37 Pornography should be discussed much younger than most parents think. The average age of exposure to pornography is 11.[28] Parents should begin teaching very young children about modesty, privacy, and self-respect. Starting with basic concepts when children are young makes it easier to transition to discussing pornography more directly later on. By age eight, children are verbal, open, curious, less embarrassed, and old enough to understand many significant concepts. If a child can access the Internet, it might be a good time to talk with them about pornography.

② 38 How can I talk to my child about pornography and healthy sexuality?

Ⓐ 38 Teaching begins by answering questions asked by children at any age simply and without embarrassment. Teaching about healthy sexuality includes providing instruction about the body and helping children understand that there are parts of the body that are kept private. Parents can effectively educate their children about pornography by creating appropriate teaching moments to discuss many of the same questions and issues presented in these questions.

27: *http://internet-filter-review.toptenreviews.com/index.html*

28: *Jerry Roplato,* Internet Pornography Statistics, *http://internet-filter-review. toptenreviews.com/internet-pornography-statistics.html*

Section 4

When children unexpectedly view inappropriate or provocative material, they often instinctively hide it from their parents out of shame and embarrassment. Taking every opportunity to bring such experiences out in the open is important. Parents can begin teaching about pornography simultaneously when teaching about the body. For example, if a child picks up a book that illustrates personal parts of the human body, a parent could respond with a comment such as, "I see that picture caught your interest. Do you have any questions? Let's talk about it." Similarly, when a child views something sexually provocative or pornographic, acknowledging the material without discomfort or surprise is important. A parent might say, "I see that caught your attention. When we run across those kinds of pictures it is important to change the channel [close the book, throw it away, etc.] and then tell a parent." It is important for parents to take the time to explain why the material is inappropriate and what to do when inappropriate material is encountered. Teaching children about what to do when they see pornography is just as important as teaching children what to do if they are exposed to any other drug.

This type of communication sends a clear message to children that parents are a good resource when they have questions. Children need to see that parents know what kinds of material are available, that they are not shocked or embarrassed by it, and that they have clear rules about what material should or should not be viewed. Responding to young children openly and factually with simple statements and explanations is generally best. As children get older, additional opportunities will arise to have more detailed discussions. If the topic does not arise on its own, find ways to bring up pornography and discuss it as children get older. For additional help, see the Resources section of this manual

---

Q 39   How should I respond if I discover my child or teen is viewing pornography?

A 39   First and foremost, stay calm and do not overreact. A child or teen's openess is going to be

influenced by his ability to trust and confide in his parents. If a parent overreacts, the child will feel shamed and become more secretive. If he senses that his parents understand and love him, however, he will be more likely to communicate with them in the future. Do not be afraid to be honest and open in your discussions. See "Creating a Safe Place to Talk about Dangerous Things" by Jeffery Ford in the *Articles* section of this manual.

It is important that children understand what pornography is, and why viewing pornography is so dangerous and damaging. If a child is regularly viewing pornography, this may be a sign of addiction. Seek appropriate help if your child is regularly viewing pornography.

Do I Have a Problem?

Q 40   How can I tell if I have a pornography problem?

A 40   Simply put, an individual has a problem when he tells himself that he is not going to look at pornography anymore and then finds himself doing it anyway. Pornography addicts return to thinking about, planning for, and participating in secret behaviors that take priority over healthy and important activities. The following list may help individuals in deciding if help would be beneficial:

- Feelings that the ability to stop viewing pornography is out of control.

- Recurring patterns of "stop-start" behavior with frequent or consistent relapses.

- Continued pornography use despite possible adverse consequences and losses including time, money, job, education, marriage, and family relationships.

- Escalation of behavior including increased time spent viewing pornography, the need for increased stimulation and viewing or participating in harsher and more graphic forms of pornography.

⬧ History of lies, secrecy, deception, and living a double life in order to maintain the appearance of normality while participating in the viewing of pornography and other sexual behaviors.

⬧ Feelings of guilt, shame, and low self-worth related to one's sexual behavior.[29]

ⓠ 41 Why is it important to be open and disclose my pornography problem to someone?

A 41 Pornography addiction thrives in secrecy and often breeds feelings of shame and guilt which tend to cause the problem to escalate. Admitting and disclosing pornography use is the first step in stopping for good. Once an addict can admit and talk about the behavior, the shame and guilt often begin to dissipate. Talking to others can provide needed support, additional resources, and accountability.

In contrast, keeping pornography behavior secret can actually create more emotional arousal, which may lead to additional acting out.[30] "Asking for support is not easy, but living in recovery requires absolute honesty and the courage to ask for help. Denial, self-deception, and isolation are hallmarks of addictive behavior. These traits make it difficult to achieve lasting and stable progress in recovery without the support and perspective of others. It is important for an addict to enlist the help of appropriate and effective support people as soon as possible."[31]

ⓠ 42 Is recovery possible and what does it involve?

A 42 Recovery is definitely possible, though difficult. Those who are completely committed to doing what it takes to find and maintain recovery are successful. Keep in mind, however, that the individual must desire recovery. The basic elements of healing are:

⬧ ***Come Out of Hiding:*** Coming out of hiding and honestly disclosing the problem to a spouse and ecclesiastical leader is essential. Committing to continued honesty and transparency is fundamental to the recovery process.

⬧ ***Become Educated:*** Gain education regarding pornography addiction and the recovery process.

⬧ ***Set Boundaries:*** Set specific boundaries to avoid situations that will compromise your commitment to recovery.

⬧ ***Work a 12-Step Program:*** Find a sponsor, attend group meetings several times a week, and work the 12-Steps on a daily basis.

⬧ ***Get Therapy:*** Seek professional counseling from a qualified therapist who specializes in sexual addiction.

29: www.combatingpornography.org

30: Gail Saltz, The Anatomy of a Secret Life. (2008) Broadway House.

31: www.combatingpornography.org

> Yea, I would that ye would come forth and harden not your hearts any longer; for behold, now is the time and the day of your salvation; and therefore, if ye will repent and harden not your hearts, immediately shall the great plan of redemption be brought about unto you.
>
> —Alma 34:31

Q 43   What recovery programs and resources are available for me as an addict?

A 43   For a list of suggested books, Internet sites, DVDs, audio CDs, therapists, 12-Step programs and Internet filters, go to the *Resource* section of this manual.

Q 44   How do I find the right counselor?

A 44   Finding professional counseling is essential to the recovery process. Most individuals and couples struggling with the impact of pornography will benefit from a combination of individual, couple, and group treatment. Support groups or 12-Step programs are not substitutes for therapeutic treatment. In selecting

a therapist, the following considerations may be helpful:[32]

* What training has the therapist received in dealing with sexual behaviors and addictions? Because of the complex nature of pornography addiction, specialized training is highly desirable. Ask the therapist if he or she is a member of a national organization for treatment of sexual addiction and if he or she has received specific certification or training.

* Does the therapist specialize in sexual addiction and how many years of experience does he or she have treating these problems? Good therapists specializing in other psychological problems may not necessarily be the best for treating sexual behavior.

* Are counseling services provided for the non-addicted spouse? Involvement of the non-addicted spouse in therapy is paramount for the spouse's personal wellbeing and also for the health of the marriage.

* Does the therapist or clinic provide group therapy? Experience has shown that recovery is

---

32: See www.combatingpornography.org

enhanced when individuals participate in group therapy.

◆ What does the therapist believe that the effects of viewing pornography are? Therapists often have varying opinions regarding whether the viewing of pornography and engaging in related sexual activities are problematic behaviors. Make certain that the therapist you are seeing shares your beliefs and value system.

◆ Does the therapist believe that pornography use can be classified as an addiction? Therapists who do not believe pornography is addictive will probably not be as effective in treatment.

◆ What steps are considered necessary to recovery? Some therapists do not believe recovery is possible or do not exhibit a strong understanding of what recovery requires.

◆ How does the therapist define recovery and measure success in treating those who view pornography? Discovering how a therapist defines recovery can also help gauge the effectiveness of treatment.

Q 45 How do I "stay clean" or avoid relapse?

A 45 Addictive tendencies do not completely go away. Nevertheless, for many individuals who diligently work the steps of recovery, the behavior is kept in check and they never act out again. This is often referred to as recovery.

Maintaining recovery generally involves continuing to work the 12-Steps, setting and keeping boundaries, and having some permanent form of accountability through participation in a recovery program with a sponsor, a religious leader, or friend. Prompt and complete honesty in admitting any slips of behavior is critical. Those who avoid relapse are generally those who recognize that they are still addicts and are vigilant in continuing to apply the tools of recovery. They also learn to recognize negative emotions and thought patterns leading to compulsions to act out on

their addictive behaviors. They address emotional needs by making necessary adjustments and reaching out to others for support long before those needs turn into addictive behaviors and acting out.

Q 46 How does viewing pornography affect me and my relationships?

A 46 Viewing pornography can distort realistic views of healthy sexuality, lead to the objectification of women, and promote sexual gratification as a top emotional priority. Insensitivity to a partner's personal needs and feelings are often a hallmark of relationships where pornography is involved. Even though pornography may be viewed in secret, the inability to connect with a partner and with loved ones is often felt by all.

Because pornography involves emotional, chemical, and physical stimulation, it can reset the brain in such a way that normal, healthy sexual experiences become unsatisfying and unfulfilling. Increasingly extreme or deviant sexual acts are often required to bring about sexual satisfaction. As a result, pornography addiction frequently destroys healthy marital relationships and can lead to sexual acting out with oneself and others, including other immoral behavior. Some statistics indicate that the likelihood of infidelity is increased by 300% where pornography is involved, and 55% of divorces in the United States occur at least in part as a result of pornography use.[33]

Pornography use destroys trust and respect and can make the user emotionally and physically unavailable to his partner. Pornography becomes a counterfeit attachment, drawing attention and time away from other relationships, such as with a spouse or girlfriend. Additionally, addicts turn to pornography to satiate emotional needs and to numb uncomfortable or painful emotions. This progressive behavior chokes the life out of healthy emotional, sexual, and spiritual intimacy between individuals.

33: See Jill C. Manning, PhD Congress Report

Section

4

Section 4

Q 47 How does my viewing pornography affect my spouse or loved one?

A 47 Not only does viewing pornography damage relationships, it can also have a direct and destructive effect on the well-being of a spouse or loved one. Pornography addiction can destroy a spouse's sense of being uniquely important to their partner.[34] Many spouses report feeling a sense of betrayal, having low levels of self-esteem, having decreased trust in their partner's commitment to the relationship, feeling a diminished sense of security, and experiencing reduced marital satisfaction.[35]

These negative emotions can manifest themselves in many ways. Wives may try to overcompensate in the hopes of regaining their husband's attention or approval. Anorexia or other eating disorders are common among spouses of addicts, along with an unhealthy sense of responsibility for the success of the marriage and the addict's behavior. Spouses may swing between feelings of anger, hatred, anxiety, and unhealthy compulsions to protect their partner and marriage from humiliation. The feelings of hopelessness may even escalate to thoughts of self-harm or suicide.

Pornography addicts frequently exert pressure on their spouses to keep the issue secret. Many spouses feel trapped in an unhealthy kind of isolation because they are unable to discuss their feelings or receive necessary needed support and help. Without appropriate help and counseling, the emotional, physical, and spiritual health of the addict's spouse may be in as much danger as the addict himself.

Q 48 How does my viewing pornography affect my children?

A 48 Pornography causes a change in the way the user relates to others—especially to their children and spouse. The pornography user learns a simple, one-sided sexual response which eliminates intimacy. The user actually loses his ability to emotionally connect with others. Instead of warmth, empathy, and compassion, the user interacts with family members with detachment and criticism. He is emotionally unavailable. This can be very damaging to children.

Q 49 Does discovering or disclosing a pornography addiction generally result in divorce?

A 49 In some cases, discovering or disclosing a pornography addiction may eventually lead to divorce. Some statistics indicate that 55% of divorces are related in some way to pornography. It is much less likely to result in divorce if the problem is disclosed by the addict rather than discovered by the spouse. A large number of couples are able to find recovery and healing for the addict, the spouse, and the relationship. Several factors increase the probability of being able to heal the relationship, as outlined in the next answer.

Q 50 As a recovering addict, what can I do to heal and strengthen my marriage?

A 50 Both the person addicted to pornography and the spouse must find their own recovery before any significant progress can be made toward healing the relationship. Pornography addicts frequently discourage their spouses from talking about the problem, getting counseling, or attending a 12-Step program. There is an instinct to keep the problem private in an attempt to protect the marriage. In reality, keeping the problem quiet feels safer and more comfortable (i.e., less volatile) but is often very damaging to both the addict and the spouse. As difficult as it is, a recovering addict who truly wants to heal and strengthen the marriage should do everything

---

34: Ibid.

35: A.J. Bridges, R.M. Bergner, & M. Hesson-McInnis, (2003). "Romantic Partner's Use of Pornography: Its Significance for Women." Journal of Sex & Marital Therapy, 29, p 1–4; Bergner, R. M., & Bridges, A. J. (2002). "The Significance of Heavy Pornography Involvement for Romantic Partners: Research and Clinical Implications." Journal of Sex & Marital Therapy, 28, p 193–206; Schneider, J. P. (2000). "Effects of Cybersex Addiction on the Family: Results of a Survey." Sexual Addiction & Compulsivity, 7, p 31–58. Cited in The Impact of Internet Pornography on Marriage and the Family: A Review of the Research, August 2005, Washington, D.C.

he can to encourage his spouse to reach out and get help for herself.

Once both partners are committed to consistently working their own recoveries, trust generally will slowly return to the relationship. Hope and optimism will grow. This does not mean, however, that the rest of the journey will be easy. During this time, both qualified counseling and individual recovery programs are usually necessary. Understand that pornography addiction often causes a substantial amount of emotional and relational trauma for the spouse. It is important that an addict allows his spouse time and space to heal at her own pace. An addict should be sympathetic to his spouse's feelings of anger, frustration, ambivalence, and hurt. As an addict makes an effort to strengthen the relationship and work on his individual recovery, the three recoveries (his, hers, and ours) begin to support and complement one another. Specific actions that can be taken by the addict to help strengthen the marriage include the following:

- Fully commit to completing all necessary elements of recovery.

- Disclose past behavior. By postponing disclosure or confessing a little bit at a time out of the fear that the spouse "can't handle everything," the healing process is often impeded and the resulting hurt prolonged. It may be wise to consult with a therapist or sponsor before making the full initial disclosure.

- Continue to promptly disclose any behavioral slips. Honesty and openness (transparency) are essential. Most spouses report that although relapses are difficult to deal with, secrecy and lies are intolerable. Graphic details are not necessary, but the spouse should know the type

Section

4

of slip, the duration, severity, and frequency of acting out.

⬦ Set realistic expectations about the recovery process. Change takes time. Recognize that the marriage takes time to heal.

⬦ Recognize the trauma a spouse may be experiencing. Reach out to the other person, try to alleviate her workload, and spend time together doing activities that can help rebuild the relationship (walking, gardening, cooking, etc.).

⬦ Encourage the spouse to get counseling and support. Attending counseling as a couple is essential.

Spouses of Pornography Addicts

Q 51 Typically, how does a spouse respond when they find out about a pornography problem?

A 51 Feeling intense hurt, sadness, low self-worth, betrayal, anger, or even hatred is common.[36] It is important for spouses to recognize how they are responding, emotionally, and to find a trusted friend or family member or ecclesiastical leader with whom they can share these feelings and seek support. It is also important to honestly share those feelings with the addicted spouse.

Keeping things in perspective is important. Having a pornography problem does not negate everything good in the addicted spouse. Still, it is a significant, serious problem and should not be minimized. Remembering positive experiences can help provide motivation to work through the difficult times ahead and apply the

necessary effort to save the marriage. It is helpful to try to be calm and compassionate. On the other hand, feeling responsible to change the addict's behavior or lashing out in anger is not helpful. The addict's spouse needs help and support as she works through her emotions and sets appropriate boundaries. Getting help may help to ensure the emotional well-being of the spouse and will aid in repairing the marriage relationship.

Watch the video, "Women Are Not to Blame for Sexual Addiction" and "Impact of Pornography" on SA Lifeline website. (www.salifeline.org)

Q 52 Why can't my spouse just stop viewing pornography?

A 52 Pornography is addictive. Once the addiction is established it is extremely difficult to quit and it is almost impossible to stop without outside help.

Q 53 How is the pornography addiction of a spouse or loved one likely to affect me personally?

A 53 Many spouses of addicts feel a sense of betrayal, fear, anger, trauma, isolation, and abandonment after discovering the immoral behavior and addiction. It is common for the addict's spouse to avoid telling others about the addiction, hide her feelings, or pretend that nothing is wrong. She often feels a great deal of pressure to protect the addicted spouse and preserve the image of normalcy. As the addict's spouse withdraws, it is common for her to feel increasingly lonely and hopeless. Depression and even thoughts of suicide may result.

Discovering a pornography/sexual addiction can start a chain of devastating emotional responses. Many spouses of addicts experience intense anger, while others respond by feeling numb and listless. Thoughts such as, *How could this happen to me?* or *What did I do to deserve this?* are common. Many spouses have feelings of guilt or a false misplaced sense of personal responsibility for the pronography/sexual addiction. Spouses often experience feelings of low self-worth

36: Bridges, A. J., Bergner, R. M., & Hesson-McInnis, M. (2003). "Romantic Partner's Use of Pornography: Its Significance for Women." Journal of Sex & Marital Therapy, 29, p 1–4; Bergner, R. M., & Bridges, A. J. (2002). "The Significance of Heavy Pornography Involvement for Romantic Partners: Research and Clinical Implications." Journal of Sex & Marital Therapy, 28, p 193–206; Schneider, J. P. (2000). "Effects of Cybersex Addiction on the Family: Results of a Survey." Sexual Addiction & Compulsivity, 7, p 31–58. Cited in The Impact of Internet Pornography on Marriage and the Family: A Review of the Research, August 2005, Washington, D.C.

and fall into thinking, *This wouldn't have happened if I had just been a better wife*, or *if I were just more attractive or sexy, this wouldn't be a problem*. This type of thinking is often followed by feeling the need to fix the problem and the belief that some action on their part, such as working harder to be pleasant or losing weight, will make the problem go away. When such efforts to fix the problem do not work, feelings of fear, anxiety, hopelessness, and despair increase. Fear and uncertainty about the future—*What is going to happen? If I were to leave the marriage, what would I do? What about the children? What about our marriage?*—can become overwhelming.

As emotional well-being deteriorates, spouses often fall into counter-productive behaviors or dangerous coping mechanisms. Spouses commonly try to be the policeman by constantly monitoring the addict or trying to manage his recovery. They frequently become obsessed with looking for "evidence" by checking their spouse's email, reading their journal, looking for unusual charges on credit card statements, or checking the calls on their spouse's cell phone. Many develop eating disorders such as anorexia, bulimia, overeating, or undereating. Serious depression is very common. Hopeful feelings like *We have finally gotten to the bottom of this and will put this behind us forever* alternate with feelings such as *There is no hope for ever getting out of this endless cycle*. The addict's spouse may wonder what is wrong and why she feels "crazy"—so out of control.

ⓠ 54 How is the pornography addiction of a spouse likely to affect our relationship?

Ⓐ 54 Discovering that your spouse is addicted to pornography can turn your world upside down. Many spouses of addicts feel deeply hurt, betrayed, angry, ashamed, numb, sad, depressed, or helpless. Many initially worry that they will never be able to trust their husband again. Spouses often feel uncertainty and fear for the future. The cycle of feelings experienced is very similar to grieving for the death of a loved one and may include the following symptoms: (1) shock, (2) disbelief or denial, (3) anger, (4) bargaining, (5)

depression and then, finally, (6) acceptance of the reality of the problem. Acknowledging, accepting, and allowing those feelings to take their course are important steps. Addicts frequently withdraw and disconnect from relationships. The addict may exert pressure on the spouse to protect his secrecy. It is crucial for spouses of addicts to get help, regardless of whether the addict himself approves.

ⓠ 55 As the spouse of a pornography addict, what can I do to find healing for my damaged relationship?

Ⓐ 55 It is just as important for the spouse of an addict to reach out and get help as it is for the addict. This means developing a strong support network, getting appropriate counseling, participating in a 12-Step program, and having a sponsor. If both parties are willing to do their part in working toward recovery, often trust can be rebuilt over time and the relationship can begin to heal. The initial focus, however, needs to be on individual recovery. While many spouses of addicts want to jump in and work on fixing the marriage relationship, working to heal the marriage can be ineffective and even counterproductive as long as the addiction and its effects on the addict's spouse are active and unresolved. It is like pumping air into a tire that has a hole in it. As long as the hole is there, any air pumped into the tire will just leak out. The hole in the marriage needs to be repaired first as each individual gets help. Repairing the marriage relationship will come later. Counseling from a qualified therapist who specializes in sexual addiction is often useful in this process.

Spouses of addicts frequently fall into behaviors that are counterproductive to the recovery process. They may try to control or compel the addict's recovery. On the other extreme, they may be so afraid of "rocking the boat'" that they will not set boundaries to protect themselves or set consequences if those boundaries are crossed. Relationships have the greatest chance of healing if the spouse focuses on her own individual recovery and well-being rather than obsessing about her husband. The spouse of the addict also needs to set clear boundaries and expectations with the addict as well as establish consequences if the boundaries are crossed.

56 How do I find hope and healing for myself as the spouse of a pornography addict?

A 56 The spouse of an addict can do many things to more effectively handle any difficult emotions and trauma. The following are basic elements to healing that many have found helpful:

- *Break the secrecy:* Develop a support system and find others to safely confide in. This may include a parent, a close friend, a religious leader, and a therapist.

- *Become educated:* Learn about the nature of pornography addiction. While spouses of addicts can support recovery, it is important to understand that the addict is responsible for his own addiction and it cannot be fixed simply by trying to control the addict.

- *Practice self-care and set boundaries:* Slow down and allow time before making life-changing decisions. Prayerfully set boundaries defining unacceptable behavior in order to protect your emotional, physical, and spiritual well-being. Make time for daily physical and spiritual care.

- *Get therapy:* Seek appropriate personal and marital counseling.

- *Find a 12-Step program:* Network with the spouses of other addicts. Work the 12 Steps of recovery and find a sponsor.

57 What programs and resources are available for me as the spouse of a pornography addict?

A 57 For a list of suggested books, Internet sites, DVDs, audio CDs, therapists, 12-Step programs and Internet filters, go to the *Resource* section of this manual.

58 How do I balance my need for support and healing with my desire to maintain my spouse's anonymity?

A 58 For the spouse of a pornography addict, getting the support and help needed is particularly difficult because doing so involves disclosing the addict's behavior to someone else, thus breaking anonymity to some degree. One of the most serious side effects of a pornography addiction for the spouse of an addict is that she can either consciously or subconsciously be manipulated into remaining quiet and suffering in silence. It is important to realize that although the addict has control over his actions, he has no right to control his spouse's behavior. The addict's spouse must feel free to build a safe support network, to attend recovery meetings, and to seek appropriate counseling. The decision about how much information to disclose and to whom should be made with sensitivity and discretion. Many women find it helpful to share what they are experiencing with a trusted friend, family member, ecclesiastical leader, sponsor, or support group. Indiscriminate disclosure of a pornography addiction is not advisable and can result in adverse consequences for children and others involved.

Dating and Pornography

For more help read related stories on pages 82-87 of this manual, and see the Handout *Pornography and Dating*.

Q 59 Why should I discuss pornography with the person I am dating?

A 59 In varying degrees, virtually everyone will have some exposure to pornography, which affects their views of sexuality. This may range from casual exposure to serious addiction. Given the breadth of widespread promiscuity in society, it is important to discuss how each individual in a serious dating relationship views and will deal with pornography, regardless of whether the person has previously had a problem. Openly discussing pornography can safeguard individuals and relationships. A person can be (1) currently addicted, (2) previously addicted but now in recovery, or (3) never addicted with minimal exposure to pornography. By determining the category the other person in the dating relationship falls into, an individual can gain valuable insight concerning how to proceed appropriately with the relationship. Even if there has been minimal exposure, it is important to openly discuss pornography and set necessary boundaries to prevent future problems.

For those who have had or currently have a problem with pornography, it is very important to discuss this with any person they seriously date. Pornography use is extremely addictive and can frequently reoccur unless significant preventive measures are taken. By talking about this problem early in a relationship, individuals can learn to develop open communication and set appropriate boundaries that will safeguard both people, help guide relationship decisions, and create a safe, trusting environment.

Q 60 When should I discuss pornography with the person I am dating?

A 60 Some people have suggested bringing up pornography by the second date. While that is probably too soon for many, here are a few questions to help guide determinations:

- Are you "exclusive" (i.e., boyfriend and girlfriend)?

- Is the relationship such that you can talk or have already talked about other significant personal issues?

- Are you looking to advance your relationship by becoming engaged or married?

- Does your partner know and trust you enough to disclose and discuss personal challenges?

For those who cannot answer "yes" to any of those questions, it may be too soon. For those who can answer "yes" to one or more questions, now might be an appropriate time. For those who can answer "yes" to all questions, it is definitely time to discuss pornography. Discussing pornography before becoming engaged is very important.

Q 61 How should I discuss pornography with the person I am dating?

A 61 There is no easy way to bring up this topic. One approach is simply to ask about his experience with pornography. Another way is to initially share a personal experience or talk about a related article and then move into the topic. It is important to ask

Section

4

Section 4

what the other person's experience with pornography has been. Discussions might include when and where pornography was last viewed and what the response was. Ask what is being done now to protect against pornography addiction. If an addiction has previously existed, ask what was done to stop viewing pornography. Did the person see a counselor or attend 12-Step meetings? Ask about relapses. If there is a problem, it is common to receive a vague, incomplete, deflective, or less-than-honest answer. For those who have any reason to think they are not getting a complete story, trust those instincts and bring the topic up again at a later date—or consider ending the relationship. A dating partner who has difficulty telling the truth about his pornography experiences has the potential to become a spouse who does not tell the truth about it after marriage.

Q 62   What should I do if I suspect someone I am dating has a pornography problem?

A 62   The answer is simple: talk to him. Discuss your concerns or suspicions with him. Consider using the questions from *Pornography & Dating,* in the *Handout* section to guide these discussions or see *www.salifeline.org*. Be careful about the speed at which the relationship progresses until recovery is solidly underway. As always, encourage anyone addicted to pornography to fully disclose his problem and get appropriate help.

Q 63   How is dating someone with a pornography addiction likely to affect me?

A 63   Pornography causes a change in the way the user relates to others. The pornography user learns a simple, one-sided sexual response which effects feelings of closeness and intimacy. This escalates into a loss of the ability to emotionally connect with others. Instead of warmth, empathy and compassion, the user often interacts with emotional detachment and criticism. He is emotionally unavailable, and may even suggest that this detachment is the fault of the person

he is dating. This can be very damaging to your self esteem and confidence.

Q 64   What will likely happen if I choose to marry someone with a pornography addiction who is not working on recovery?

A 64   Pornography addiction is not a problem that is fixed by marriage and marriage won't make the problem easier to fix. Additionally, this addiction will always escalate. A person with a pornography addiction cannot build a healthy relationship. Their ability to be unselfish, compassionate, and emotionally available is severely compromised by their addiction.

Q 65   As a recovering pornography addict, what factors should I consider in dating?

A 65   Although graphic details are not necessary, it is important to tell the other person the nature and extent of behavior related to viewing pornography early in the relationship. Consider setting boundaries regarding the speed with which the relationship progresses based on your recovery progress. It is frequently recommended that an addict be well along in the recovery process at least 7–12 months before entering into a serious relationship.

Q 66 What factors should I consider when deciding whether to continue a relationship with someone who is addicted or has been addicted to pornography and is in recovery?

A 66 Recognize that those addicted to pornography can change their lives, but do not underestimate the power of pornography addiction. Love for the addict requires exercising patience and setting appropriate healthy boundaries at all stages of the relationship. This may require (1) waiting to move forward in a relationship, (2) deciding to end a relationship, or (3) setting and abiding by specific rules and guidelines regarding a relationship's progression. An important factor in deciding whether to continue in a relationship is whether the person is in recovery or is actively seeking recovery from his pornography addiction. It is frequently recommended that there be at least 7–12 months of solid recovery before proceeding seriously forward. It is important that individuals understand what recovery looks like and are able to identify whether their loved one is in the recovery process.

If the addict is currently viewing pornography, it is important to proceed slowly with the relationship or to give serious consideration to ending the relationship. Be careful not to confuse emotions with the best course of action. Dating a person with an active pornography addiction can have very serious and unexpected emotional consequences. Carefully weigh the risks of continuing in such a relationship. Carefully evaluate whether the other person acknowledges that he is addicted, is willing to take the steps required to recover, and is actively doing everything in his power to overcome this addiction. It is important to talk with trusted individuals, become educated regarding pornography addiction, and set boundaries. Additionally, attending counseling and 12-Step support groups may be helpful.

Q 67 What should I do if I am dating (or have dated) someone with a pornography problem and I am currently struggling with negative thoughts about myself and my appearance?

A 67 It is not uncommon to experience some kind of trauma after being in a close relationship with a pornography addict. Common problems may include obsession with personal appearance, feelings of low self-worth, decreased self-confidence, a feeling of spiritual darkness and abandonment, a decreased ability to trust and form healthy relationships with men, and acceptance of unhealthy or abusive behaviors as normal.

If someone who is dating or has dated a pornography addict starts to experience any of the feelings listed above, it is important that she talk with someone. She may consider seeing a counselor and attending a 12-Step program. Getting support from a professional counselor who understands the impact of pornography addiction is important. Talking with friends or family who can offer support and help put things in perspective is also helpful.

Leaders

Q 68 How can I educate those in my stewardship about the dangers of pornography?

A 68 There are several obstacles to combating pornography, including a lack of awareness surrounding the nature and magnitude of the problem, embarrassment discussing or dealing with pornography openly, and a lack of understanding about whom pornography affects. Leaders can be instrumental in effectively educating those within their sphere of influence by taking opportunities to arrange appropriate and effective presentations and discussions on the topic. The goals of these presentations may include helping others understand the following:

Section

4

Section 4

- The nature and magnitude of the pornography problem, as well as how it affects them, their friends, and their loved ones.

- The need to confront the problem directly and openly.

- The addictive nature of pornography and what steps must be taken to find recovery.

- The effect pornography has on dating and potential marriage relationships.

- Potential warning signs that a pornography problem exists.

- The negative effects that an addict's behavior can have on loved ones.

- The need for individuals struggling with pornography addiction to disclose their problems and seek appropriate help.

- The need to be sensitive to and supportive of those who are affected by pornography addiction—both those addicted and their afflicted spouses.

- How to find the help and support needed for addicts and their loved ones.

- The need to be proactive in teaching children about healthy sexuality, the dangers of pornography, taking steps to keep the home safe, and how to deal with pornography issues as they arise.

Q 69 As a leader, how can I best help an individual with a pornography addiction?

A 69 Many individuals are afraid to take the initiative to confess a pornography problem. Directly asking specific questions, such as, *When was the last time you viewed or were exposed to pornography?* can effectively help open the discussion. "Yes" or "no" questions such as, *Do you have a pornography problem?* are less effective and generally do not lead to further discussion.

If an individual is struggling, encourage him to meet with you regularly. Consistent accountability regarding the specific recovery actions being taken and the length of his sobriety are important. When questioned, individuals may respond that they are not viewing pornography, but fail to fully disclose other "acting out" behaviors, such as regular or periodic masturbation. Provide encouragement as they work their recovery program.

Encourage individuals to (1) be transparent in disclosing behavior to their spouse and ecclesiastical leader, (2) become educated, (3) set boundaries, (4) get therapy, and (5) attend appropriate 12-Step meetings.

> *O Lord, wilt thou grant unto us that we may have success in bringing them again unto thee in Christ.*
> —Alma 31:34

Q 70 As a leader, how can I best help the spouse of an individual with a pornography addiction?

A 70 Pornography addiction often has devastating effects for the spouse of the addict. It is common for spouses to experience significant trauma, yet fail to get adequate or appropriate help, support, and counseling. Recognize and watch for serious potential side effects such as depression, eating disorders, or thoughts of suicide. It is also common for the spouses of addicts to start questioning their faith in God as they struggle to understand why He would allow this to happen. Listen to and validate the spouse's feelings. Become educated regarding the effect an addict's pornography addiction can have on his spouse. Strongly encourage the afflicted spouse to (1) continue seeking support from trusted individuals, (2) become educated about the addiction, (3) set boundaries and practice self-care, (4) get therapy, and (5) attend appropriate 12-Step meetings. Take the time to learn about all of these actions and what is required for a pornography addict to achieve and maintain recovery, and what is necessary for his wife to find her own recovery.

Section

4

🍁 71   *What is an* **enabler?**

A 71 An enabler is someone who shields an addict from the negative consequences of his behavior. While the enabler is most often a relative or spouse, the enabler can potentially be a priesthood leader. An enabler in the same home with the addict might intend to protect the addict, the family, or herself from embarrassment. She might lie to others, or minimize or disregard clear evidence of addictive behavior in an attempt not to rock the boat or make things worse. Often an enabler sincerely believes that he or she is acting in the best interest of the addicted spouse or family member. The reality, however, is that enabling behavior is harmful to the enabler, the addict, and others around them. Enablers usually are unable to see that their decisions are making the situation worse rather than better. It is absolutely essential to understand that enablers are not responsible for, and cannot control, the addict's behavior. Nevertheless, their choices and actions make it possible for the addict to continue his acting out without experiencing the full consequences of his behavior. When the addict finally has to face the full consequences of his actions, he is much more likely to seek full and effective treatment for his addiction.

🍁 72   *How can leaders avoid becoming enablers to those dealing with pornography and sexual addiction?*

A 72 A priesthood leader most frequently becomes an enabler when he suggests a solution for the addict's "little problem," and then proposes a course of treatment that primarily consists of daily prayer, scripture study, and better time management. The priesthood leader often does not understand that viewing pornography results in a "behavioral or natural addiction" and involves not just spiritual trauma but also serious mental and physical trauma that is not easily healed without the involvement of a qualified therapist and the support of a 12-Step fellowship.

Nevertheless, by assuming that this is just a bad habit that can be overcome through sincere personal effort, the leader misleads the addict, spouse, and parents into thinking that what they are doing is entirely sufficient for full recovery. They may dismiss professional therapy and 12-Step groups as unnecessary and oftentimes "overkill" for dealing with a valiant priesthood holder's problem. The pornography user sticks with his resolve for a few months until he and the priesthood leader conclude that the "little problem" has been overcome and further check-ins are unnecessary. Without full addiction recovery work, the pornography user will lose his resolve and return to his pornography addiction, which evolves into acting out sexually.

Priesthood leaders must remember what pornography actually is. Pornography is Satan's perfect weapon to mock and scorn the divine gifts of our bodies and our ability to procreate. In addition, it is highly addictive, so it can rob us of our free will. The damage it can cause to our souls is far greater and more serious than damage done by a Word of Wisdom infraction. Voluntarily viewing pornography, because it is a calloused disrespect of our divine nature, can cause a severing of our ties to God, leaving the natural man totally alone in the world without peace and hope. Viewing pornography is never a little problem.

Read the letter from an addict to a bishop on page 11 of this manual.

Q 73   What have church leaders recently said to the brethren of the church about the seriousness of the plague of pornography?

A 73 Gordon B. Hinckley, as President of the Church of Jesus Christ of Latter-day Saints, in the priesthood session of General Conference October 2004 said the following in a talk titled *"A Tragic Evil Among Us"*:

"(T)he matter of which I speak . . . is like a raging storm, destroying individuals and families, utterly ruining what was once wholesome and beautiful. I speak of pornography in all of its manifestations. Now, my brethren, I do not wish to be negative. I am by nature optimistic. But in such matters as this I am a realist. If we are involved in such behavior, now is the time to change. Let this

be our hour of resolution. Let us turn about to a better way."

President Hinkley continues his talk, quoting from a letter he received from a wife whose husband was involved in pornography throughout their marriage, "Please warn the brethren (and sisters). Pornography is not some titillating feast for the eyes that gives a momentary rush of excitement. [Rather] it has the effect of damaging hearts and souls to their very depths, strangling the life out of relationships that should be sacred, hurting to the very core those you should love the most."

President Hinkley lovingly continues his counsel, "(Y)ou, too, know enough of the seriousness of the problem. Suffice it to say that all who are involved become victims. Children are exploited, and their lives are severely damaged. The minds of youth become warped with false concepts. Continued exposure leads to addiction that is almost impossible to break. Men, so very many, find they cannot leave it alone. Their energies and their interests are consumed in their dead-end pursuit of this raw and sleazy fare. The excuse is given that it is hard to avoid, that it is right at our fingertips and there is no escape.

"Suppose a storm is raging and the winds howl and the snow swirls about you. You find yourself unable to stop it. But you can dress properly and seek shelter, and the storm will have no effect upon you. Likewise, even though the Internet is saturated with sleazy material, you do not have to watch it. You can retreat to the shelter of the gospel and its teaching of cleanliness and virtue and purity of life.

"I know that I am speaking directly and plainly. I do so because the Internet has made pornography more widely accessible, adding to what is available on DVDs and videos, on television and magazine stands. It leads to fantasies that are destructive of self-respect. It leads to illicit relationships, often to disease, and to abusive criminal activity.

" Now brethren, the time has come for any one of us who is so involved to pull himself out of the mire, to stand above this evil thing, to "look to God and live" (Alma 37:47). We are men of the priesthood. This is a most sacred and marvelous gift, worth more than all the dross of the world. But it will be amen to the effectiveness of that priesthood for anyone who engages in the practice of seeking out pornographic material.

"The Holy Ghost shall be thy constant companion, and thy scepter an unchanging scepter of righteousness and truth; and thy dominion shall be an everlasting dominion, and without compulsory means it shall flow unto thee forever and ever. (D&C 121:45–46) How could any man wish for more? These supernal blessings are promised to those who walk in virtue before the Lord and before all men.

"If there be any within the sound of my voice who are doing so, then may you plead with the Lord out of the depths of your soul that He will remove from you the addiction which enslaves you. And may you have the courage to seek the loving guidance of your bishop and, if necessary, the counsel of caring professionals.

"Let any who may be in the grip of this vise get upon their knees in the privacy of their closet and plead with the Lord for help to free them from this evil monster. Otherwise, this vicious stain will continue through life and even into eternity. Jacob, the brother of Nephi, taught: 'And it shall come to pass that when all men shall have passed from this first death unto life, insomuch as they have become immortal, … they who are righteous shall be righteous still, and they who are filthy shall be filthy still'" (2 Ne. 9:15–16).

Elder Dallin H. Oaks of the Quorum of the Twelve Apostles in the priesthood session of General Conference April 2005 said the following in a talk titled "Pornography":

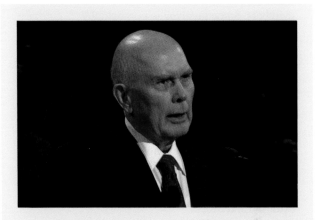

"My fellow holders of the Melchizedek Priesthood, and also our young men, I wish to speak to you today about pornography. I know that many of you are exposed to this and that many of you are being stained by it.

"In concentrating my talk on this subject I feel like the prophet Jacob, who told the men of his day that it grieved him to speak so boldly in front of their sensitive wives and children. But notwithstanding the difficulty of the task, he said he had to speak to the men about this subject because God had commanded him (see Jacob 2:7–11). I do so for the same reason.

"In the second chapter of the book that bears his name, Jacob condemns men for their "whoredoms" (Jacob 2:23, 28). He told them they had 'broken the hearts of [their] tender wives, and lost the confidence of [their] children, because of [their] bad examples before them' (Jacob 2:35).

"What were these grossly wicked 'whoredoms'? No doubt some men were already guilty of evil acts. But the main focus of Jacob's great sermon was not with evil acts completed, but with evil acts contemplated.

"Here, brethren, I must tell you that our bishops and our professional counselors are seeing an increasing number of men involved with pornography, and many of those are active members. Some involved in pornography apparently minimize its seriousness and continue to exercise the priesthood of God because they think no one will know of their involvement. But the user knows, brethren, and so does the Lord.

"One of the Savior's most memorable teachings applies to men who are secretly viewing pornography: 'Woe unto you, scribes and Pharisees, hypocrites! for ye make clean the outside of the cup and of the platter, but within they are full of extortion and excess.

'Thou blind Pharisee, cleanse first that which is within the cup and platter, that the outside of them may be clean also.' (Matt. 23:25–26; see also Alma 60:23)

"The immediate spiritual consequences of such hypocrisy are devastating. Those who seek out and use pornography forfeit the power of their priesthood. The Lord declares: 'When we undertake to cover our sins, … behold, the heavens withdraw themselves; the Spirit of the Lord is grieved; and when it is withdrawn, Amen to the priesthood or the authority of that man.' (D&C 121:37)

"Patrons of pornography also lose the companionship of the Spirit. Pornography produces fantasies that destroy spirituality. 'To be carnally minded is death'—spiritual death. (Rom. 8:6; see also 2 Ne. 9:39)

"The scriptures repeatedly teach that the Spirit of the Lord will not dwell in an unclean tabernacle. When we worthily partake of the sacrament, we are promised that we will 'always have his Spirit to be with [us].' To qualify for that promise we covenant that we will 'always remember him.' (D&C 20:77) Those who seek out and use pornography for sexual stimulation obviously violate that covenant. They also violate a sacred covenant to refrain from unholy and

impure practices. They cannot have the Spirit of the Lord to be with them. All such need to heed the Apostle Peter's plea: 'Repent therefore of this thy wickedness, and pray God, if perhaps the thought of thine heart may be forgiven thee'. (Acts 8:22)

"Brethren, you have noticed that I am not discussing the effects of pornography on mental health or criminal behavior. I am discussing its effects on spirituality—on our ability to have the companionship of the Spirit of the Lord and our capacity to exercise the power of the priesthood.

"Pornography impairs one's ability to enjoy a normal emotional, romantic, and spiritual relationship with a person of the opposite sex. It erodes the moral barriers that stand against inappropriate, abnormal, or illegal behavior. As conscience is desensitized, patrons of pornography are led to act out what they have witnessed, regardless of its effects on their life and the lives of others.

"Pornography is also addictive. It impairs decision-making capacities and it 'hooks' its users, drawing them back obsessively for more and more. A man who had been addicted to pornography and to hard drugs wrote me this comparison: 'In my eyes cocaine doesn't hold a candle to this. I have done both. … Quitting even the hardest drugs was nothing compared to [trying to quit pornography]'. (letter of Mar. 20, 2005)

"Some seek to justify their indulgence by arguing that they are only viewing 'soft,' not 'hard,' porn. A wise bishop called this refusing to see evil as evil. He quoted men seeking to justify their viewing choices by comparisons such as 'not as bad as' or 'only one bad scene.' But the test of what is evil is not its degree but its effect. When persons entertain evil thoughts long enough for the Spirit to withdraw, they lose their spiritual protection and they are subject to the power and direction of the evil one. When they use Internet or other pornography for what this bishop described as 'arousal on demand' (letter of Mar. 13, 2005), they are deeply soiled by sin.

"King Benjamin's great sermon describes the terrible consequences. When we withdraw from the Spirit of the Lord, we become an enemy to righteousness, we have a lively sense of our guilt, and we 'shrink from the presence of the Lord'. (see Mosiah 2:36–38) 'Mercy hath no claim on that man,' he concluded; 'therefore his final doom is to endure a never-ending torment.' (Mosiah 2:39)

"But the good news is that no one needs to follow the evil, downward descent to torment. Everyone caught on that terrible escalator has the key to reverse his course. He can escape. Through repentance he can be clean."

Section

4

ONE. *Sitting in a Rowboat Throwing Marbles at a Battleship* . . . .*Page 73*

TWO. *Would We React Differently to Cancer?* . . . .*Page 80*

THREE. *Discovering Hope and Healing: Part I* . . . .*Page 82*

FOUR. *Discovering Hope and Healing: Part II.* . . . .*Page 84*

FIVE. *Finding the Power to Forgive* . . . .*Page 85*

SIX. *Finding Myself* . . . .*Page 86*

SEVEN. *Discussing Pornography as a Family* . . . .*Page 87*

Section 5

Sitting in a Rowboat Throwing Marbles at a Battleship

A Recovering Sexual Addict's Story

My first experience with pornography was at age six. Six-year-olds don't have the strength or capacity to say no to an older person looking to expose them to pornography. I certainly didn't. This was especially true after I heard the enticing description of the pictures I would find in the magazine hidden out in the cherry orchard. This older person, a teenage boy in the neighborhood where my family had recently moved, understood that the pornography he showed me became a secret we shared. He formed a covert bond with me and then used that bond to coax me to an isolated location where he could molest me. These experiences flipped a switch in me at age six, and I became a sex addict.

I think a lot of people have a pretty hazy idea of what a sex addict looks like. We imagine a pudgy, middle-aged guy in a trench coat with greasy hair and twitching, crazy eyes who sneaks around and peeps at women through their bedroom windows because he can't control his sex urges. The reality, however, is that in much the same way that there is a broad spectrum of alcoholics—from apparently able and functioning members of society at one extreme to the poor inebriate passed out in the gutter in some large city at the other—there is a broad spectrum of sex addicts.

To be sure, some sex addicts do sit in dark, dingy bedrooms with the curtains drawn, surfing for pornography on the Internet for days at a time. But sex addicts are also very often some of the ordinary men, women, and children in the community around us. Some of them are your bosses or employees at work. Some of them are the people sitting with their families in front of you in the benches at church. Some of them are the kids on your child's baseball team. Although they come from all walks of life, I feel certain that most sex addicts share some common traits. First, they are miserable. Second, they wish that sex wasn't such an overwhelming part of their lives, devouring everything else. Third, I would also bet that many, if not most, sex addicts don't know that they are addicts. They think they just have a "little problem."

Addiction has been, and remains, very misunderstood. A lot of people fear that if we acknowledge that addiction is something beyond a particular person's control, we somehow give that individual a free pass to do whatever he wants in society without any accountability for the consequences. Although we have generally come to accept the reality of alcohol addiction, hard drug addiction, gambling addiction, a myriad of food addictions, and even shopping addiction, many of us honestly believe that addicts merely suffer from a deficiency of moral character. Addicts are not as righteous, are not as spiritual, are not as noble, and are not as sincere as the rest of us. Addicts, we believe,

just don't want to get out of their addiction. If addicts were truly serious and wanted to change, they would just stop doing what they're doing. Simply put, we think that addicts prefer to be the addicts that they are. We assume they like the bondage of addiction better than they like the freedom that the rest of us enjoy. They choose addiction. I absolutely disagree.

I believe the greatest misunderstanding about addiction has to do with its size and power. I hope no one seriously thinks that an addiction is like a little red devil who sits on your shoulder whispering naughty thoughts in your ear and who may be easily disposed of by a little flick of the finger. Perhaps those who have never dealt with addiction might imagine, instead, a couple of wrestlers in a ring. They are more or less evenly matched in size, weight, and skill. Sometimes one wrestler gets the upper hand; sometimes the other controls the match. The addict is one wrestler; the addiction is the other. The idea is that the addict just has to learn some moves, build some

strength, think positively, listen to his coach, and eventually he will prevail over the addiction. It's tough work, but that addiction can be whipped. Again, I flatly disagree with this perspective.

I see addiction in a different way. I see a six-year-old boy in a tiny rowboat in the middle of the ocean with a handful of marbles. A gray, armored battleship is steaming towards him. He can hear it coming, but he can't see it very well because thick fog is everywhere. He is trying to sink the battleship by throwing marbles at it. I am the six-year-old boy. My sex addiction is the battleship. Those marbles are my efforts to overcome the addiction on my own. The fog is misinformation, confusion, bias, and judgmental attitudes about my addiction. It keeps me from seeing two stark realities: (1) this battleship is enormous—as big as a football field, and (2) I am alone in a tiny rowboat trying to stop it with marbles! Because of the confusion caused by the fog, I have the idea that if I can just throw those marbles hard enough, I will eventually pierce the hull and sink the battleship. I can even hear some of my marbles pinging off the side of the ship as I throw them, so I'm convinced that I'm causing major damage. I tell myself with conviction that soon I will have conquered my addiction. But it will never happen as long as marbles are all I have to throw.

During my lifelong battle with the enemy in the ship, I kept looking for reinforcements. I talked with psychiatric professionals about my inability to control my periodic compulsions to act out sexually. The doctors shrugged and said they didn't really see sex as a problem. One told me that if I didn't like what I was doing, I should stop. I figured the doctors must not be too concerned about it, or they would have taken my pleas more seriously. I also asked for help from bishops and stake presidents. The Church leaders would assure me of the Lord's love and concern, and suggest more sincere prayer, more diligent scripture reading, and a more broken heart and contrite spirit. Apparently, I needed more repentance.

I felt the genuine empathy of these priesthood leaders and resolved to them, to myself, and to God that this time, I would prevail. I would slay my Goliath! Of course, those of us with a limited mortal perspective all had pictured in our minds a wrestling opponent of similar size, weight, and skill. One thing I also noticed was that talking with someone about my problem relieved my burden somewhat and made me more hopeful. But there was still a huge problem. Now I was sitting in my lonely, little rowboat, praying and reading my scriptures, before I once again started throwing more marbles at the battleship.

I have a friend who spent years living in emotional and mental turmoil. She had overwhelming feelings that she was unworthy of God's love, that she was a

failure as a mother and wife, and that other people were better or better off than she was. At times she considered taking her own life. One day, I was struck by the thought that I knew something she didn't.

My wife and I sat down with our friend and I talked to her about depression. I explained that oftentimes people feel debilitating unhappiness and assume that it is because of some spiritual deficiency. If I were more spiritual (or righteous, or compassionate, or goal-oriented), they reason, I would be happy. If I am not happy, it must be because of some moral or spiritual shortcoming. I told her that depression was different from sadness. Sadness is an emotion that follows unwanted or troubling experiences and events in our lives. When bad things happen, sadness is the appropriate emotional response. That's not what happens with depression.

Depression is the product of a broken brain. Something doesn't work quite right, and as a result, the depressed person is physically and mentally unable to feel and enjoy happiness. What's worse, the depressed person's emotional state may range from merely miserable on good days to intolerably painful on bad days. Whatever the root cause—missing brain chemicals or disrupted electrical impulses or something else—depression is the result. It is not a spiritual malady. It is a physical disease of the brain.

If we have a broken leg, we go to the hospital and have a doctor set the bone and put the leg in a cast. We do not seek out a priesthood holder for a blessing and then head back to the armchair in the living room for more prayer and meditation and a greater recommitment to spiritual growth. Although a blessing may be helpful for the healing of the broken leg, we

> **If** *we have a broken leg, we go to the hospital and have a doctor set the bone and put the leg in a cast. We do not seek out a priesthood holder for a blessing—and then head back to the armchair in the living room for more prayer and meditation and a greater recommitment to spiritual growth. Although a blessing may be helpful for the healing of the broken leg, we recognize that the Lord expects us to get medical help to fix our injury.*

recognize that the Lord expects us to get medical help to fix our injury.

Disease in a broken brain, however, is often treated differently. For some reason we think that a broken brain can be fixed by praying and asking the Lord to heal our unhappiness. Because I suspected that my friend suffered from depression, I told her that I thought she needed to see a psychiatric professional to consider that possibility.

My friend seemed surprised. This had never occurred to her before. I was also surprised. During all this time and throughout all her interactions with people close to her, it appears that no one before me had ever raised to her the possibility of depression. Eventually, she met with a psychiatric professional, was indeed diagnosed with depression, prescribed the proper medication and blessedly began enjoying the happiness that can occur when a brain is functioning correctly.

For years, my friend had been looking in the wrong direction for a solution to her problem. For years, she had been praying with ever-increasing fervor for the Lord to remove the burden of her misery. The Lord did finally answer her prayers, but it was not in the way she was expecting. She assumed she would get direct intervention from God. Instead, God put a friend in her path that was able to observe her and, relying on his own experience with depression, was able to convince her to seek a doctor's help.

It is my experience that addiction, sex addiction in particular, is treated in a similar way by addicts and those around them. Sexual transgressions are second only to murder in seriousness. Sexual sins are a blatant violation of God's law and therefore evidence of a deficient moral character. Sin and immorality can only be overcome by the Atonement of Jesus Christ after faith and sincere repentance, accompanied by a broken heart and a contrite spirit. In effect, God (through Christ) intervenes in the life of the sinner and purifies him of the sin. He is born again and becomes holy, without spot. The sinner repents of his sins, focusing on his direct relationship with Heavenly Father and Jesus Christ, but also confesses his sins to a Church leader. In some cases, Church discipline follows. But what about the sex addict and his sex addiction?

Like depression, addiction is in large part the product of a broken brain. One LDS neurosurgeon has documented the destructive physical effect that pornography has on the brain.[1] It eventually incapacitates parts of the brain in the same way that cocaine or alcohol can destroy an addict's ability to resist the compulsion to take drugs or other harmful

1: Donald L. Hilton Jr., MD, www.salifeline.org "Can Pornography Be An Actual Brain Addiction?"

substances into his body. Because of the neurological component of sex addiction, treating it as one would treat sexual transgression—as a purely spiritual malady—is ineffective.

A book that deals with the topic of overcoming sex addiction asserts that if lustful thoughts are permitted "to remain in our heads without dealing with [them] immediately, we begin physical, mental, spiritual, emotional, and neurological changes within us." Note that there are five types of change that lust can cause in us.

I understand now that for years I was trying to address what I thought were the spiritual issues of my problem and completely ignoring the emotional, mental, physical, and neurological components of addiction. I also wasn't enlisting the help of those most qualified to help assist me on the "non-spiritual" end of the spectrum. There is no question that I should have been looking to my priesthood leaders for help with spiritual issues and to advise me on spiritual matters. Emotional matters can be directly related to the spiritual ones, so priesthood leaders often help to deal with those as well. Once we get into mental matters, however, a priesthood leader is probably outside the area of his expertise and beyond his abilities to directly treat the problem unless he has training in that area. A priesthood leader would only treat physical ailments if he were also a physician. Neurological issues are, of course, left to the specialists.

In my view, treating sex addiction the same as sexual sin amounts to treating one, or possibly two, of the five components of addiction. It's like rendering first aid to the victim of a shotgun blast by applying focused pressure to one of the twenty or so entry wounds while he bleeds to death out of twenty or so other holes.

Over the course of my adult life, I have spoken at different times with perhaps eleven priesthood leaders about my struggles with pornography and sexually acting out. They felt for me and expressed love and concern for me as I related my shame, suffering, and frustration. All of these men suggested or insisted on treating my problem with the balm of repentance and forgiveness through the Atonement. Although I embraced their counsel, it just didn't seem to be enough to keep me from going back to my addiction. But then things changed. I have now been sexually sober for over one year. Sexual sobriety has a specific meaning to me: no form of sex with self or any other person other than spouse. Period. This is by far the longest period of complete sobriety that I have enjoyed in many years, perhaps in all my adult life. With sobriety comes serenity and happiness. I recently told my wife that for the first time in my life, I am happy without an asterisk next to the word "happy."

To what do I attribute my sobriety? Interestingly, it did not come through a greater or renewed and somehow increased commitment to spiritual abstinence from pornography and acting out sexually. I have not felt any great changing of my heart; in fact, I don't think I've ever mentioned a changed heart in my prayers during these past few months. I am no more serious about remaining sober now than I was all those other times when I committed to myself and the Lord that I would never act out again.

There is also one other thing about which I am dead certain: my heart is no more broken and my spirit is no more contrite now than it was in the past. When I was molested as a six-year-old, my heart was broken and my spirit was contrite. When I went to my bishop as a teenager to talk to him about my desire to stop lusting and acting out sexually, my heart was broken and my spirit contrite. When I put my marriage at risk and first disclosed to my wife years ago that I thought I might have a problem with Internet pornography and couldn't seem to beat it on my own, my heart was broken and my spirit contrite. When I went to meet with my bishop the next evening, my heart was broken and my spirit contrite.

Each time I met with a priesthood leader about trying to find a solution to my "problem," my heart was broken and my spirit contrite. Every time I spoke to my wife about my inability to stay away from pornography and then had to watch the pain in her face as she tried to understand, my heart was broken and

Section

5

my spirit contrite. When I finally disclosed to my wife the extent of my acting out over the past several years and again placed our marriage on the brink of oblivion, I had a broken heart and a contrite spirit. I struggle to understand any suggestion that I have not had a broken heart or contrite spirit. A broken heart and a contrite spirit pretty much describes my entire life.

So what was the difference this time around? In short, I finally came to understand that I had lost the war, and so I surrendered—not to my addiction, but to God. I gave up and turned it all over to Him. I quit throwing marbles. After the last disclosure to my wife, as I was floundering in desperate misery, unsure whether our family would remain intact, I was struck by the distinct clear impression that I needed to call a good friend of mine in another state to tell him what I had done and enlist his help. I followed the impression and made the call. My friend listened to me patiently until I stopped to take a breath, and then he told me some things that changed my life.

First, he told me that he knew exactly what I was going through at that moment, because he and his wife had dealt with the same thing nearly four years earlier. Second, he told me that my brain was broken, that I had an addiction. He said I needed to quit trying to beat it on my own because it couldn't be done. Third, he told me that there was hope for recovery and that all was not lost. Fourth, he told me about a 12-Step program called Sexaholics Anonymous (SA). He described it as a collection of admitted sex addicts who met together in groups all over the country to support each other in their quest for sexual sobriety. He phoned me several times over the next few days, each time suggesting gently that I needed to get to an SA meeting as soon as I could. Finally, he quit suggesting and just told me unequivocally to get myself to a meeting.

I went to my first SA meeting on a Friday night. There were eleven other men in the room when I arrived. I was struck by how happy they all looked. I wondered if I was in the right place. For the next hour, I listened in awe as each of these men articulately shared his struggles with sex addiction, his hopes, his successes, or his failures. It was inspiring. When it was my turn to share, I was able to talk about everything: the loneliness, the shame and humiliation, my fear that I had destroyed my marriage, the pain I had inflicted on my wife, my desire to change my life, get away from the acting out, and simply live as I knew God wanted me to live. As I spoke, the other men listened intently, many of them nodding or smiling quietly as I said things that were familiar to them from their experiences. Afterwards, I went to dinner with several of them and they explained to me how SA worked to keep people sober. I went to another meeting on Saturday morning, and another on Monday morning and another on Tuesday evening and another on Wednesday evening and another on Friday evening. I have attended meetings less frequently but regularly ever since.

A remarkable thing about SA is the way it exposes addicts' secrets to the light of day in a safe way and in a safe place. One of sex addiction's biggest hooks to control the addict is secrecy. Like an infection, the shame and fear that accompany the addict's actions, thoughts, and behavior remain hidden inside where they can fester and grow cankerous. The more miserable and isolated the addict becomes, the more he feels compelled to medicate away his misery by acting out with his drug—even knowing that the fix will only last a short time and that greater misery and isolation will follow.

When I go to those meetings, I am able to bring all the secrets out into the light. We don't speak in a salacious way, but respectfully and with reverence to the fact that the addiction is bigger and more powerful than we are. We acknowledge repeatedly during the meetings that we are powerless over our addiction, that our lives have become unmanageable, and that only God can restore us to sanity.

We call each other between meetings. Sometimes we call because we are having a rough day dealing with the addiction or some resentment that could give rise to a desire to act out. Sometimes we call because we want to reaffirm to someone else our intention to remain sober for another day. Sometimes we call just

Section
5

to check in and say hi, because the act of checking in helps us get our heads straight, reminds us how good sobriety feels, and disrupts the addiction's pattern of leading us into isolation and resentment. I have called other members in the program when I was having trouble. Other members have phoned me at times.

Once I got a call at 11:30 p.m. My friend didn't tell me he was having a bad night, but I could tell. We chatted for a few minutes about nothing in particular, expressed our appreciation for each other, and said good bye. That short phone call helped him stay sober that night, and helped remind me of how grateful I was to God for finally, after so many years, so many tears, and so much pain, leading me to a place where I can recover from my addiction.

I have a sponsor now. He is one of the most remarkable men I know. His faith knows no bounds. His enthusiasm never stops. His smile is infectious. His insights are always just what I need to hear. He and I share the same profession. Like me, he is a husband and a father. And he has been in the SA program and sober for over seven years.

I also serve as a sponsor to several men who are new to the SA program. Working with them is an opportunity for me to share the experience, strength, and hope that have come to me as a blessing of recovery. It is a chance for me to save lives and save marriages. I love to see that tiny spark ignite in their sad, tired eyes when they attend their first SA meeting—when they start to hope that maybe they've found what they were searching for—maybe this is the solution to the nightmare. I smile and tell them with confidence, "This will work—if you're willing to work it!"

One of the many mottos of the 12-Step programs is "One Day at a Time." I work at staying sober and in recovery one day at a time. I recognize that I am still a sex addict and that I will always be a sex addict. That is my reality. But I also realize that if I do what is necessary, I can remain in recovery, which means staying completely and absolutely sober. That is what I intend to do. Sexaholics Anonymous, with God's help, inspiration, and strength, will help me do that.

I need to tell you about how the picture of my addiction inside my head has changed now. I still see myself in a tiny rowboat and the battleship is still out there. But now, the fog has dissipated so that I can see the enormous size of my enemy and know that this battle is very, very lopsided. It is nothing at all like two wrestlers in the ring. I know that I will lose if I just sit there by myself in my rowboat with my marbles.

But now I also see a bunch of other rowboats surrounding mine—not many, but enough—and recognize my friends from SA. They have blowtorches and drills and metal-cutting saws. They tell me to stick with them and they will show me where to cut and drill and torch to slowly dismantle that battleship piece by piece. They tell me, "We know how to chop this thing up, because we've done it before ourselves." Sure enough, I can see their battleships lying in pieces in the distance. Some are neatly stacked, while others are in a bit of disarray. But it's clear that their battleships are destroyed and they are now out there helping others like me dismantle theirs. One of my good friends in the program recently told me with a smile, "It takes an addict to help an addict." I believe that.

Finally, what is the power source that all these cutting tools plug into so they can be used to chop up my battleship? There is no question in my mind: it is the power of a loving God who is mindful of me, my wife, and my family; a God who wants us to return one day into His presence. That is my hope.

Would We React Differently to Cancer?

A Woman's Experience in Healing from Her Husband's Pornography Addiction

My husband has been a pornography addict since he was thirteen. He struggled with this addiction all through high school. He was able to stay away from it for several years, but in our second year of marriage, while I was pregnant with our first child, the problem returned, and we have battled it ever since.

I have known about my husband's addiction for over nine of our nearly eleven-year marriage. In that time it has taken a terrible toll on our family. Both of us have experienced major losses because of this addiction: personally, professionally, emotionally, and spiritually. For many years we repeated an endless cycle: he would tell me it wasn't a problem anymore, and I would believe him—or at least pretend I did—while wondering why something felt so wrong in our marriage and our home. When things would finally get so bad I could not ignore it any more, I would confront my husband and he would once again admit to viewing pornography. He would then work to conquer the addiction by "controlling his thoughts," exercising self-discipline, and increasing his spirituality. Despite his efforts, he was never open about discussing his

pornography addiction with me or anyone else. He said that even just discussing it could trigger an "outbreak," so I was afraid to bring it up. I desperately tried, against my better judgment, to believe that pornography wasn't a problem anymore (still wondering why things felt wrong in our marriage) until something would bring it to the surface again and the cycle would start over.

We tried counseling for a while but it "didn't help him," or it "took too much time and money," and he would eventually quit. I read about 12-Step programs, so we bought some workbooks and tried working on those on our own. We even moved to a different state to try to get into a better situation where it wouldn't be such a temptation, but none of these things were enough to bring lasting change.

Meanwhile, I felt like I was going crazy. Something still seemed wrong in our marriage. I would feel anxious and panicky and then told myself it was nothing. I never caught my husband looking at it or had any proof, so I just convinced myself that I was being suspicious and paranoid. Whenever the problem surfaced, I blamed myself. I felt like it was my fault for not being attractive enough or just "letting myself go" after having children. I tried going to counseling but my husband strongly discouraged it. I thought about going to a 12-Step group, but I had kids and didn't feel like I had time for that. For years I didn't tell a single person about my husband's addiction. I felt like I needed to ask my husband's permission before doing anything. I was afraid of him and yet afraid of losing him. I felt completely alone.

This fall, through a series of circumstances (I believe it was God's hand in my life) I ended up talking to a woman who had been through a similar experience with her husband. I had believed that pornography hadn't been a major problem for my husband for the past several years, but this summer I was starting to become uncomfortable again with the way he was acting and treating me. I attributed the changes to stress at work but still felt in my gut like something wasn't right. This woman told me that, from her experience, it sounded like my husband was not in recovery from his addiction and never had been. This was very hard to hear but I recognized it as the truth. She offered to become my sponsor (a mentor who guides someone through the process of recovery) and I started working a 12-Step program through S-Anon, a 12-Step group for spouses or family members of sex addicts.

Initially, my husband was very unsupportive, even antagonistic, and resented my efforts at recovery. I started setting boundaries with him about what I was willing to live with. He eventually admitted that pornography had still been an issue for him for the past several years and it was actually getting worse. He reluctantly agreed to go to 12-Step meetings, but still was mostly just trying to placate me. After much prayer, I finally reached the point where I told him that he needed to be completely honest and transparent with me about his addiction and to actively work on recovery from his addiction by attending Sexaholics Anonymous, getting a sponsor, and seeing a counselor for at least a year. If not, I was unwilling to stay in our marriage. My husband finally reached rock bottom and started working on his own recovery in earnest.

Since then we have seen miracles happen, both individually and in our relationship. Although recovery is difficult and time consuming, for the first time I can see a clear path to healing, a path that we have already begun. My husband is truly a different person: he is open and honest about his addiction, both with me and with others. He willingly attends his 12-Step meetings and works closely with a sponsor. He actively wants to help any others who may be struggling with this addiction that came so close to destroying our marriage and our family. He is more concerned with maintaining sobriety, helping others, and rebuilding our relationship than with saving face, protecting himself, or maintaining secrecy.

For many years, we tried to deal with this problem on our own. I struggled to forgive my husband and maintain the appearance of a normal family while my husband struggled to "control his thoughts" and resist temptation. The problem was that he was an addict—he had lost control over the addiction and no longer had the power to resist it on his own. Despite his many sincere attempts to stop and despite being aware of the major personal losses we had both suffered as he pursued his addiction, he inevitably fell back into pornography, leaving both of us in despair. I battled severe depression and at one point almost became suicidal.

For so many years both of us wanted the addiction to be removed. We wanted it to just go away. We would try to increase our spirituality, make some life changes, even major changes like moving to a different state, or otherwise attempt to fix things, but we weren't willing to surrender everything and just ask God what we needed to do. We always held something back. We would only consider changes that fit into the framework of what we thought was needed: as long as they didn't require talking about it with other people, as long as we wouldn't be risking possible embarrassment, as long as it didn't require me to find a babysitter for the kids, as long as it wasn't too expensive or time consuming, as long as it didn't involve some silly support group. This time I finally realized, with the help of my sponsor, that I have to surrender everything. Only when I am willing to turn my life over to God and do what He requires with exactness can I find peace and healing.

So what does God require? I feel he has required me to fundamentally change the way I live my life and look at this issue. I have to stop focusing on my spouse and how I think he needs to recover. I recognize that this isn't my fault: I didn't cause it and I can't fix it. Instead I turn my efforts to being in a healthy place myself (physically, emotionally, and spiritually) and trying to do what God wants me to do each day. I focus on healing from the trauma that I have experienced and doing what I need to do to feel safe and healthy. I actively work on recovery every single day. Each week I attend two S-Anon meetings, group therapy, and a counseling appointment.

I continue educating myself about pornography addiction and recovery. I practice self-care, taking time to slow down and meet my physical, emotional, and spiritual needs. I set boundaries or limits with my husband to protect myself from unacceptable behavior. I lovingly convey my support of his efforts toward recovery, but make it very clear that I will not live with addictive behavior. If this seems like a big commitment, it is. It takes a significant amount of time and effort.

The problem is, I haven't found anything else that works—and, believe me, I have spent nine years trying to find some easier way. When it starts to seem like too much work, I ask myself, "If one of us had cancer, would we decide to not do chemotherapy treatments because it was too time consuming?" The effect of pornography in our lives has been just as devastating as cancer. Working at recovery is time consuming and frequently painful, but at least for us it has been every bit as necessary as chemotherapy for treating cancer. Recovery is a lifelong process. Just like all healthy living, it is a lifetime commitment that you work at every single day.

Discovering Hope and Healing: Part I
A Young Man's Experience Dealing with Pornography While Dating

I was introduced to pornography when I was around eleven years old. I loved it and I hated it from the beginning. I think I soon became an addict. I grew up in what I call a "religid" family and culture. My

mom cried when she found out I drank Dr. Pepper. There was no way I could tell my parents that I was viewing pornography, though I desperately wanted help. I felt there was no one I could trust with this shameful secret.

When I got into my twenties, it was still there and even more of a struggle. I confessed to and worked with at least nine different bishops. Nothing worked. The longer this addiction went, the worse it got. The pornography was more graphic. I started acting out with girls; some of them I was dating, some of them I was not. I stayed away from a few girls through the years that I really liked, thinking once I got this under control then I could date them. It didn't happen. I saw no hope. I couldn't stop. Even if I could stop, what I heard in the culture I grew up in is that no girl would or should ever want to marry me because I had been involved in pornography at some point in my life. I was full of toxic shame. I was getting more and more depressed. I was having thoughts that if there was really no hope of marrying someone in my faith, then why try and fight this anymore. Why not just go with it and live like many other people do.

About this point in my life, a miracle happened. A friend introduced me to my first 12-Step group. It was great. I found my first glimmer of hope. By chance (or maybe not), within a month I met the woman I am married to today. We lived in different states and started dating long distance. We were falling in love pretty quickly with our only regular contact being hours of phone calls. I knew I had to tell her so she could run away and not have to deal with me. I did. It was very difficult, for both of us.

She didn't run away though. She did talk to her bishop who I am very grateful to. He didn't tell her to run away either. He said he had a friend and neighbor who was a top therapist in treating sex addiction. When she told me about this I couldn't wait to get started. If there was something out there that would really help me get this out of my life I wanted to do it. Whatever it took, I wanted to do.

I had tried so many times to stop by myself. I should have been able to stop if I was just strong enough or had enough faith or worked hard enough or read my scriptures enough, right? Even with the help of a bishop, it had never worked.

I soon moved to Utah, started therapy, and found a number of 12-Step groups. It was hard. Recovery was great though. I couldn't believe what I was learning. I like to put my recovery process into two categories, though they are completely intertwined: (1) my spiritual recovery and (2) my functional recovery.

My spiritual recovery meant learning a new gospel of Jesus Christ. I had been taught and internalized the God of the Old Testament. A God of justice, vengeance, war, punishment, and fear. There is no hope in that and no recovery in that. In recovery, I learned the gospel of the New Testament. Jesus has come. He loves me. He has paid for my sins. He is a God of mercy, love, grace, and forgiveness. He does not speak to me with fear. He speaks to me with love.

I could speak for hours on the details of this wonderful, amazing journey. I have been learning this new gospel for over five years now, and I plan on learning it the rest of my life. My functional recovery has been through therapy: learning about family systems and roles, shame, the drama triangle, the limbic system and the prefrontal cortex, codependence, fear, objectifying, and boundaries. I have learned to recognize, analyze, and share my feelings. I have a set of tools to deal with triggers, whether sexual, mental, or emotional.

I remember thinking in my first month of therapy while learning some of these functional recovery items, "Wow, people can actually do things differently? People can communicate differently than my family did and does? People can communicate differently than my community and culture did and does?" I never thought there was any other way.

Like my spiritual recovery, I am still very engaged in anything that I can learn therapeutically: books, therapists, recovery groups, and men's groups. I think there is enough that I will have plenty to do for the rest of my life. I love it and I am so grateful that I can continue this journey with God.

Section 5

I am not where I was five years ago. I don't deal with the same triggers I did five years ago. Most of my triggers are not sexual in nature. Don't get me wrong; I am powerless over sex and lust. I just know I can surrender that to God and he has the power to handle it, and I just need to be humble enough to let him handle it. I am in an amazing place. There is mercy, grace, and forgiveness. There is love and kindness and patience. These things are not based on tasks or time or acts. God loves you. Jesus Christ loves you. Today. Right now. No matter where you are in your life. They Love You! You are okay. You are a good person.

To start on this journey, all you have to do is be like Alma the younger and countless other individuals and groups of people in the scriptures. He merely thought of Jesus Christ, of whom his father had taught him, and then he prayed "Oh, Jesus, thou Son of God, have mercy upon me." After repentance and healing, God and His Son Jesus Christ gave Alma the strength that enabled him to go forward and become a great man.

Believe God can heal you. Believe He will heal you. Let the Atonement work in your life. Find someone who will help you let the Atonement work in your life, and you let the Atonement work in theirs.

Discovering Hope and Healing: Part II

A Young Woman's Experience Dating an Addict

I am sharing my story because I think it is important to offer a realistic picture of the peace and joy that is attainable in a marriage even when a pornography addiction exists. That peace and joy has only come for us as we have committed to do the hard work of therapy, recovery, looking at ourselves, surrendering our weaknesses, being completely honest with each other, and forgiving ourselves and others. Too often, we hear of the outcomes of divorce, separation, and family breakups that come with addiction. While those are true and very painful, there are also stories of hope and happiness.

I met a man over five years ago and soon realized I was in love. I felt differently than I ever had before.

We talked so easily about everything. We shared the same interests. Shortly after we met, he disclosed that he had recently begun attending a 12-Step group for pornography addiction. I remember quickly thinking back to what I knew about addiction, what I knew about pornography, and what I even knew about sex, which wasn't much.

Somehow I didn't feel the urge to run away. I still loved him. What this did was heavily put the brakes on any decisions I wanted to make regarding our relationship. We lived in separate states. I had looked into moving to where he lived and that didn't feel right anymore. Neither did talking about marriage. Neither did breaking up though. Through a respected leader, I was introduced to a therapist who specialized in pornography addiction. I called him to get some information. I wanted to know if people could change and how long it could take.

To make a long story short, it soon became clear that we needed to be near each other and begin therapy if we were going to continue dating. So, this man quit his job, left his family and friends, and moved to Utah. I appreciated his honesty with me and his willingness to give up whatever he needed in order to try to make some positive changes. We started therapy that month and were told it was probably wise not to make any major decisions for a year or so. That took off the pressure of even thinking of marriage. We figured we'd both be better for going through this, even if we didn't stay together or end up getting married.

We were one of very few dating couples in the therapy program. Most were married, and most wives found out that their husbands were addicts after they were married, either because he finally disclosed it or because he was caught. I felt like some of these women thought I was nuts for going through this without even the commitment of marriage. But my boyfriend and I had a very strong relationship of trust. I trusted him. I trusted that he would be truthful with me. This didn't mean that he would be perfect and never have a slip up, but his willingness to be honest was important.

We set similar boundaries as the other couples. If he did have a slip up, he had twenty-four hours to tell me about it. It was hard for him to tell me, but he did each time. Oftentimes, I would get upset and take it personally at first. We were in therapy, first as a couple for six weeks, then me with other women and he with other men weekly for a year and half. I met individually with a therapist once a month and through that whole process realized I had a lot of my own problems to work on, whether my boyfriend was an addict or not. I learned of some family secrets through this process. I believe that through my own therapy and recovery—working on me without worrying about him—I was able to process and work through my own fears.

We were engaged about eight months after we began therapy and married three months later. We continued in weekly therapy our first year of marriage. We both "graduated" from our therapy programs. My husband still attends a weekly 12-Step group and we attend a monthly couples group. Recovery is a regular word in our home, as is addiction. These words no longer bring fear or panic to my mind like they once did. They bring peace and hope.

At first, marriage and sex added an interesting dynamic to our relationship. Our "normal" newlywed struggles were often attributed to addiction rather than just to life, and we have learned to put those into perspective. I believe I am a better person for having gone through this together, and for starting our marriage on a healthy, trusting foundation. That's my story up until now. We have a great working marriage and continue to learn together. We appreciate and love each other. We definitely have our ups and downs. Some days we feel like we're back where we started, but we're not even close to that. We are equals and both feel so lucky to have each other. We both feel that our therapy has given us new tools, not only in our marriage relationship but in parenting, in other relationships, and in meeting life's joys and challenges.

Finding the Power to Forgive

A Young Woman's Experience after Dating a Pornography Addict

I had dated a lot prior to meeting John but had never really met anyone that I thought I could marry. When I met John, it was obvious that things were different. The relationship began to progress quickly and I was beginning to feel pretty confident that this was the guy I wanted to marry. Things were moving steadily along until I discovered John had a pornography problem. John expressed a strong desire to overcome his addiction and progress in the relationship. I still loved him and wanted things to work out, so instead of breaking up, I decided to take things slowly, confident that he would find recovery and our relationship would work.

I wanted him to recover so badly that it made it very difficult to recognize and accept the fact that although he continually expressed a desire to recover, John was not exhibiting the type of commitment and actions necessary to actually find recovery. I finally realized that without substantial changes, John would not improve, and those changes were not happening.

After breaking up, John and I continued to have contact. I still loved him and was concerned about his well-being. After speaking with a therapist, I began to realize the need to set firm boundaries, not only in terms of my interaction with John, but also in terms of communicating what I needed to tell our mutual friends who were constantly inviting us to the same parties and activities, which was difficult for me.

After the break up, I began to experience a lot of unexpected side effects—an obsession with losing weight, exercising, and trying to look perfect. I struggled with my faith in God. God knew what would happen, so why didn't he protect or warn me sooner? I felt like I had been betrayed by someone I trusted and began to develop a distrust of men and relationships. I felt everything about my world had been shaken in ways I never could have anticipated.

Recognizing that I needed help, I attended 12-Step meetings. Working the steps and regularly reporting to a sponsor helped me to set boundaries and identify and overcome negative thought patterns and behaviors. It also helped me recognize that I had to forgive John. After breaking up, I felt a number of things John had done were very wrong and it was difficult not to feel some resentment. Forgiving John was a process and it took time. As I worked the 12-Steps, I realized that I not only needed to forgive John, but I also needed to ask John for his forgiveness. That was really difficult. I finally met with John and simply explained that I had felt resentful towards him and I needed to apologize. The relief and peace I felt was overwhelming. He didn't apologize or express any remorse for anything he had done at the time, but I knew I had taken an important step in my own recovery.

Time has passed and we are friends. We interact comfortably in groups and have casual conversations. I am very careful to keep my boundaries in place. I still feel a sense of loss for the relationship that might have been, had the situation been different, but I am comfortable and confident that my life is going the way God wants it to go and that is enough for me.

Finding Myself

The Recovery Story of a Man Struggling with Pornography Addiction

I was truly lost. At least I felt that I was. I had allowed my addictions to turn me into a shell of my former self. I knew that I was cheating myself, my family, and most importantly the Lord from my best self. It had been years since I enjoyed the constant companionship of the Spirit. I was fighting a dual addiction of pornography and prescription pain medication. These addictions coupled with my business travel had spun me into a life of secrecy. I lived a life of deception and half-truths. I can remember hiding out from the world in hotel rooms wishing for it to all end somehow. I felt I was teetering on the edge of a dark abyss from which there could be no return.

I can remember during that time that there was only one prayer which I prayed with any real fervency. I prayed that the Lord would open the road to repentance for me before I left this life. It scared me that the drive to come forward and confess was slowly fading. The longer I justified my actions and prolonged my repentance, the more numb I became to how it affected me. I was absolutely certain that admitting my guilt would result in the loss of everything of value in my life.

It was then that the Lord reached out and provided an answer to my prayer. A miracle was received and confession followed. There were certainly moments of doubt and shame, but they were always reinforced by an outpouring of blessings. The reemergence of the Spirit in my life felt like the dawning of a new day and a new me. It was amazing to feel the lines of communication open again with my Father in Heaven. In my addictions, I had allowed myself to be convinced that the Lord wouldn't listen to me anymore. I was certain that I wasn't worthy to even talk with Him. However, it soon became clear that Satan had persuaded me to overinflate my feelings of dread and worry. Those that I feared would condemn my actions were actually the most compassionate and forgiving.

I attribute much of my healing and learning to the PASG (Pornography Addiction Support Group) program. Walking into my first meeting was one of the hardest things I've ever done. Now, I value the brotherhood I feel with others who are working through their own problems and challenges. There is an undeniable spirit in the PASG meetings. The openness and humility present during the meetings foster true healing. Each week, there are key steps discussed on how to cope spiritually and to avoid common pitfalls. Action steps are outlined to create a clear plan of recovery. The sharing portion of the meetings help all in attendance learn from others' victories and setbacks. Relationships of encouragement and trust are forged to help provide strength during moments of weakness.

I am happy to say that upon writing this account, I have enjoyed over fourteen months of sobriety from all my addictions. My relationship with my wife is stronger and more honest than at any time during our sixteen years of marriage. I have been blessed to enter again into the temple worthily and to partake of the sweet Spirit there. I now enjoy the blessings of fellowship and service that once seemed so distant.

I still have challenging days, but I feel equipped with a spiritual arsenal to combat these challenges. I am extremely grateful that this blessing of healing is available to all who seek it. I am blessed to have been given another chance. Through the help of my Church leaders and the PASG program, I have a better understanding than ever of the gifts of the

Atonement. I am hopeful that I can work to pass along this message to others as well.

Discussing Pornography as a Family

A Family Story

I attended a Relief Society meeting where a lesson had been presented on protecting children from pornography. I had brought home a handout on how to talk to children about pornography, which I discussed with my husband. I was a full-time, stay-at-home mom and was very aware of what my children were doing and I felt that I had excellent communication with them. I was sure that my children had no exposure to pornography, but my husband and I decided to talk to our children about this subject that evening anyway. I felt that the children were probably a bit young for this conversation and I was quite certain that they had no exposure to pornographic materials, but thought that this was a good conversation to periodically have.

My husband and I have two sons, ages twelve and ten, an eight-year-old daughter and a younger four-year-old son. We decided that we would meet with the three older children and let our youngest son watch his favorite video. I led the discussion, starting by briefly talking about what pornography is and telling about the first time I saw pornographic material. I then asked the children if they had ever seen pornography. The twelve-year-old immediately spoke of a time when a picture popped up on the computer screen and how this image kept flashing in his memory and he didn't know how to stop it. It was obvious that this was something that deeply bothered him and that he hadn't known what to do about it or how to bring it up to talk about it. We then talked with the kids about ways to stop a disturbing image or thought from being in your memory.

I then asked our second son if he had ever seen any pornography. He said no and then his younger sister chimed in, "Well, what about that time I walked into the living room where you and your friend were on the computer looking for pictures of naked women?" We took this opportunity to talk about the dangers of pornography and how important it is to avoid it. My husband and I plan to meet with the children every three months, as a group and individually, to talk about the question, "When was the last time you saw pornography?" I was shocked at the fact that, without this conversation, my children would have never shared their exposure to pornography with me or my husband.

ONE. *The Effect of Pornography on the Spouse of an Addict.* . . . .*Page 91*

TWO. *Talking to Youth and Children about Pornography* . . . .*Page 94*

THREE. *Creating a Safe Place to Talk About Dangerous Things.* . . . .*Page 98*

FOUR. *Can Pornography Use Become an Actual Brain Addiction?* . . . .*Page 101*

The Effect of Pornography on the Spouse of an Addict

Geoff Steurer, MS, LMFT

It's not uncommon for well-intentioned observers to inquire about the fuss being made over pornography. Many of them assume that pornography consumption is a victimless pastime. Their line of thinking generally supports the notion that a man who views pornography in isolation is not hurting anyone. They even debate the question of whether or not this same man is hurting himself by viewing pornography.

I would like to challenge these assumptions by sharing how pornography use damages not only the individuals who view it, but especially the wives and girlfriends of these same men. I will also include suggestions for how women affected by their partners' pornography use can cope as they and their partner begin the journey toward wholeness.

In all my years of counseling individuals and couples, I have never seen any other behavior produce a pattern of pain and misery to an individual and his marriage as predictably as pornography. Let me briefly outline the pattern as I see it.

First, long before his wife discovers his pornography use (either by his own disclosure or by her catching him), he will begin to slowly change into someone who becomes more self-centered, irritable, moody, and impatient. He will spend less focused time with his family, seek out more distractions, begin to mentally and even verbally devalue his marriage, become critical of his wife's body and character, feel more spiritually empty, and experience more internal stress.

He will become more restless, more dissatisfied with his work, and easily bored with things that used to interest him. He will also become more resentful and blaming when things don't go his way.

This transformation may take years, depending on how often the individual views pornography. If he only seeks it out every few months, he may be able to fool himself that the aforementioned challenges are situational and will pass with time. For the person who views pornography more frequently, each viewing produces more disconnection from the man he could become. The repeated viewings and subsequent self-deception deepen this transformation over time. This gradual erosion eventually creates confusion and strife in the marriage. Although each case is different, most wives who knew nothing of their husband's secretive pornography consumption have told me they felt like something was "off" in their relationship with their husband. They usually second-guessed themselves, many of them even reflexively blaming themselves entirely for the disconnection in the marriage.

If undisclosed pornography use has the potential to produce much confusion and pain in a marriage, one can only imagine the level of difficulty imposed on a wife when these secretive behaviors are actually brought to light.

Shock, denial, anger, rage, depression, self-loathing, isolation, and fear are some of the emotions a woman experiences when she learns of her husband's secretive sexual behaviors. Virtually every woman I've worked with has experienced deep shame, embarrassment, and humiliation. Unfortunately, partners will often suffer privately and become more disconnected and isolated from their support systems. Even if they initially react in anger, most of the pain becomes "sorrow that the eye can't see."[1]

Most men who reveal their secretive behaviors feel the relief of not having to carry the secret anymore. Ironically, the crushing load once carried by the addict is transferred to the wife. Burdened by this new and unwelcome challenge, she typically experiences profound fear, anxiety, and confusion.

Many scholars have noted that women betrayed by their husband's pornography use experience symptoms associated with post-traumatic stress disorder, a condition that is equated with feelings of powerlessness, intrusive thoughts and memories, and efforts to avoid the triggers associated with the traumatic stressor. Like war-torn soldiers, these women live in fear that something will remind them of the painful memories associated with the betrayal of pornography. They often become hyper-vigilant—checking computer histories and cell phones and obsessing over ways to stop their husband's pornography use.

The stress associated with discovering a husband's pornography addiction can produce sleepless nights, food issues (both overeating and undereating), traumatic flashbacks, crying spells, and feelings of hopelessness for the wife. The physical exhaustion related to these stressors can cause a once perfectly healthy woman to begin under-functioning in her various roles.

Dr. Shondell Knowlton, a marriage and family therapist in Farmington, Utah, has compared the experience of a wife learning of her husband's secret pornography use to tipping over a cart of neatly stacked apples. Dr. Knowlton says that when the metaphorical apple cart gets dumped over, the order and predictability of life is scattered in all directions. Energy previously used for other things is rerouted to gathering, cleaning, sorting, and restacking the apples. This process is fraught with disorder, confusion, and humiliation.[2]

Many women believe they will automatically recover from the trauma of their husband's pornography use when he stops looking at it. It's easy

to imagine how this would be the case. If the behavior that is causing the pain goes away, then the pain goes away, right? Yes and no.

Yes, the pain will decrease as a husband commits to ending his pornography consumption and begins to live an authentic life free from the damaging effects of this addiction. On the other hand, if women affected by their husband's pornography use don't consciously work to undo the effects of his behavior, they could continue to hold onto unresolved fear, resentment, anger, and grief.

Another comparison helps to clarify this point. If a woman is a passenger in a car driven by her out-of-control husband and he steers the car into a tree, it's unlikely she'll get back into a car with him without some sort of reassurance that he'll be more safe. Even if he takes driver safety classes and pays fines, she will still struggle to know if he's going to protect her. She will need to work through her own emotional reactions, trauma, and feelings of powerlessness associated with the injuries caused by her husband's irresponsible driving. The couple will need to work through the impact of the husband's pornography addiction on each of them individually and then work on the relational impact caused by his behavior.

Women who discover their husband's pornography use will benefit from doing some emotional first-aid to help stabilize them so they can set themselves up to do their long-term healing work. I will outline some of the most helpful first steps women can take when they discover their husband's behavior. I will then briefly

---

1: LDS Hymn #220 "Lord, I Would Follow Thee"
2: This was taken from the following CD set: https://www.myexpertsolution. com/experts/keskinner/products/331373/

explain what is involved in long-term recovery for women affected by their husband's pornography use.

First-Aid

1. Physical self-care is probably the most overlooked aspect of early recovery for women. Trauma is mostly experienced in the body. The body is designed to protect us from danger. If an individual experiences a serious threat to his or her safety (emotional or physical), the body will become tense, flooded with adrenaline, and have difficulty calming down. To ignore the body is to ignore one of the greatest resources for healing. I have found that women who make physical self-care a priority heal much faster from the impact of their husband's secretive behaviors. Many women find that getting more sleep, eating healthy foods, exercising, meditating, stretching, soaking in warm water, and slowing down to nurture their physical body can help them shift out of survival mode so they can think clearly.

2. Spiritual grounding provides feelings of peace, hope, and reassurance in the face of so much uncertainty. Meditation, prayer, seeking comfort and counsel from words of ancient and modern prophets, and counseling with Church leaders allow women access to power and strength beyond their own. Seeking a priesthood blessing from a home teacher, family member, or Church leader is another powerful source of comfort and strength for many wives. Some women feel forsaken by God when they've been betrayed by those closest to them. Spiritual healing is essential, even if it takes time. Some women find it hard to attend church and spend time with others when they feel so low and vulnerable. If this is difficult, remember that being around others can be healing even if you don't reach out and share. Also, it can help to spend time where spiritual feelings are easier to access, such as visiting peaceful locations in nature or listening to uplifting music.

3. Emotional expression is critical throughout all stages of recovery, but especially in the early stages.

Many women find it helpful to write their feelings in a new journal that they have the option of throwing away at a later date. Emotions can be so strong early in this process that some women worry about putting raw feelings in their regular journal. It's important to have the freedom to express feelings in a healthy, non-aggressive way. Recognize that no feeling is inappropriate. Feelings come and go like the waves of the sea, so it's important to give them full expression and movement. Holding on to any strong emotion with the hope that it will disappear only keeps it stuck. Talking with others can also help, which is explained in the next item.

4. Connecting with others who can help is also difficult to do, but offers tremendous benefits. It is not recommended that a woman who learns about her husband's behavior broadcast her pain to just anyone who will listen. Instead, it's important to identify a few key individuals who: (1) will keep confidences, (2) can provide a safe place to talk, (3) won't negatively judge her or her husband, and (4) can offer some support and direction. It can be beneficial for the long-term stability of the relationship for a woman to inform her husband that she will be speaking to specific individuals about her struggles. Helpful individuals often include ecclesiastical leaders, therapists, parents or siblings, 12-Step support groups, therapy groups, and close friends.

5. Simplifying life is certainly a goal for most people, but this is an excellent reason to begin. This is the ideal opportunity to begin saying "no" to extra commitments, evaluating the schedule, and looking for things to cut out. Dealing with the trauma of betrayal is so physically and emotionally exhausting that everything that used to feel easy will suddenly feel impossible. It's important to keep a simple structure in place so there is order and predictability in life. However, a frenzied pace only functions as a distraction and eventually catches up in the form of more hopelessness and feelings of failure, and powerlessness. Helping

others can create a sense of purpose as well. It is better to slow down and prioritize those things that will bring the greatest peace, joy, and comfort.

6. Education is critical in the early stages of recovery. There are many good resources available to help women understand the scope of the problem. A readings list for partners is available on www. LifeSTARstgeorge.com. Education can help validate common feelings and clear up misconceptions about addiction and recovery. One of the best resources available to partners is the book *Your Sexually Addicted Spouse* by Barbara Steffens and Marsha Means.

Long-term Healing

Healing from the effects of a husband's pornography addiction is best compared to grief, loss, and bereavement. The discovery of a partner's secret sexual behavior can cause a woman's life (as she knew it) to flash before her eyes. Recovering from this loss is a process of understanding the shock and anger, processing the sadness of what was lost, and moving toward acceptance of the new life. The new life may or may not include a husband who is committed to long-term recovery. Regardless of that outcome, it's still critical for women to do the long-term work of healing from the impact of secret pornography use.

Talking to Youth and Children About Pornography[3]

Dan Gray, LCSW (Licensed Clinical Social Worker)

Today's youth are bombarded by explicit images—most of them carnal and lustful. But because of the complexity and delicate nature of sexual issues, many parents are reluctant or embarrassed to discuss the subject with their children. Consequently, many youth are schooled by misguided friends or corrupt media and often develop inaccurate views about sexuality. Those views may lead to inappropriate behaviors.

We want to teach our youth the law of chastity and help them avoid the pain of immorality. So what can parents and priesthood leaders do? We need to discuss with our youth the sacred nature of human intimacy and help them understand and bridle the feelings associated with that intimacy.

If we teach only about misused sexuality, our youth might become insecure and uncertain. We may inadvertently convey this confusing message: "Sexual thoughts and feelings are bad, sinful, and wrong—save them for someone you love." Youth who receive only negative messages about sexuality may conclude, "Since sexual feelings or urges are bad, and I feel them very strongly, I too must be bad." This kind of thinking can result in feelings of low self-worth, unworthiness, and shame, leaving the young person feeling distant from the Spirit.

Open conversation can prevent much of this confusion. As we talk to our youth about the sacred nature of our bodies and procreation, we'll be able to help them understand and avoid the spiritual, emotional, and physical dangers of pornography.

The Body Is Sacred

The media often portray an unrealistic view of how our bodies should look and what they represent. This view leads people to see the body as an object rather than an essential part of a person's soul. Accepting this view can lead to near worship of the "perfect body" and, when one doesn't match up, to self-loathing.

Rather than let the media teach our youth this destructive worldly view, we can teach them that our bodies, in all their varieties, are wonderful, God-given gifts, created to provide joy and fulfillment. In 1913 Elder James E. Talmage (1862–1933) of the Quorum of the Twelve Apostles stated: "We have been taught to look upon these bodies of ours as gifts from God. We Latter-day Saints do not regard the body as something to be condemned, something to be abhorred. We regard [the body] as the sign of our royal birthright. It is particular to the theology of the Latter-day Saints that we regard the body as an essential part of the

---

3: This article was originally published in the July 2007 issue of Ensign, p 48–51. (Republished with permission of Dan Gray, LCSW.)

soul."[4] This understanding can help youth look on their own bodies and the bodies of others with deep respect.

Elder Jeffrey R. Holland of the Quorum of the Twelve Apostles also articulated the sacred nature of our bodies:

"We simply must understand the revealed, restored Latter-day Saint doctrine of the soul, and the high and inextricable part the body plays in that doctrine.

"One of the 'plain and precious' truths restored to this dispensation is that 'the spirit and the body are the soul of man'.[5]

"Exploitation of the body (please include the word *soul* there) is, in the last analysis, an exploitation of Him who is the Light and the Life of the world."[6]

Sexuality Is a Gift

In addition to being blessed with physical bodies, we are also given the sacred power of procreation. Our Heavenly Father has sanctioned the act of sexual expression in marriage and allows married couples to experience pleasure, love, and fulfillment in that expression. President Spencer W. Kimball (1895–1985) stated: "In the context of lawful marriage, the intimacy of sexual relations is right and divinely approved. There is nothing unholy or degrading about sexuality in itself, for by that means men and women join in a

process of creation and in an expression of love."[7] Our sexual drives—when expressed appropriately—should therefore be seen as wonderful, sacred gifts.

There was provided in our bodies—and this is sacred—a power of creation, a light, so to speak, that has the power to kindle other lights. This gift was to be used only within the sacred bonds of marriage. Through the exercise of this power of creation, a mortal body may be conceived, a spirit entered into it, and a new soul born into this life.

This power is good. It can create and sustain family life, and it is in family life that we find the fountains of happiness. It is given to virtually every individual who is born into mortality. It is a sacred and significant power, and I repeat, my young friends, that this power is good.

Much of the happiness that may come to you in life will depend on how you use this sacred power of creation.

— ELDER BOYD K. PACKER
"Why Stay Morally Clean," *Ensign*, July 1972

4: *In Conference Report, Oct. 1913, 117*

5: *D&C 88:15*

6: *Jeffrey R. Holland, "Of Souls, Symbols, and Sacraments" BYU Devotional, Jan. 12, 1988*

7: The Teachings of Spencer W. Kimball, *ed. Edward L. Kimball (1982), 311*

Section

6

The Harmful Effects of Pornography

One of the things that can corrupt this sacred power is pornography. President Gordon B. Hinckley has said that through its use "the minds of youth become warped with false concepts. Continued exposure leads to addiction that is almost impossible to break."[8]

Many individuals, even some professional counselors, excuse or even condone viewing pornography as harmless behavior. They rationalize that it is "normal" and causes no harm when done in seclusion and privacy. This same rationale is used in excusing the accompanying practice of masturbation. So how do we respond when youth ask, "What is it about pornography and masturbation that is wrong?" The following four thoughts may be helpful in addressing this question.

⬧ It defiles souls—souls for which Jesus Christ atoned. The body is part of the soul; therefore, when we look upon the body of another person to satisfy our own lustful desires, we are disrespecting and defiling the very soul of that person as well as our own. Elder Jeffrey R. Holland warned us of the consequences of rationalizing or taking these things lightly:

In trivializing the soul of another (please include the word body there) we trivialize the atonement, which saved that soul and guaranteed its continued existence. And when one toys with the Son of Righteousness, the Day Star Himself, one toys with white heat and a flame hotter and holier than the noonday sun. You cannot do so and not be burned.9

Pornography defiles and degrades the body and spirit. We need to respect the sacred nature of others and of ourselves.

⬧ It can keep us from reaching the fullest potential of our souls. Our Heavenly Father has created our bodies and our spirits. He knows how they work together best. He knows what will help us reach our potential and what will hinder our progress. He knows what we should take into our bodies and what we should leave out. Prophets have taught us that putting pornographic images into our minds is detrimental to our spirit and that in so doing, we jeopardize our ability to have happiness and joy. If, however, we follow the Lord's directives from the scriptures and prophets, we will be able to experience the fullest potential of our souls.

⬧ It can become addictive. Repeatedly viewing pornography—especially when coupled with masturbation—can become habitual, even addictive. The addiction is established when a person becomes dependent on the "rush" of chemicals the body creates when one views pornography. He or she learns to depend on this activity to escape from or cope with life's challenges and emotional stressors like hurt, anger, boredom, loneliness, or fatigue. This dependency becomes very difficult to break and sometimes escalates to sexual encounters outside the bonds of marriage.

⬧ It creates unhealthy expectations for marriage. When a person views pornography and becomes aroused, the body experiences the same arousal patterns as in a real sexual encounter. When this behavior is repeated frequently, the body and the mind become conditioned to certain sexual images and behavior, which can create unrealistic and unhealthy expectations of what a sexual relationship should or will be. Such expectations carry over to marriage, creating pain, distrust, conflict, confusion, and betrayal of trust between spouses.

Having Unceasing Virtue

The Lord offers tremendous blessings to those who have clean and virtuous thoughts coupled with charity: "Let virtue garnish thy thoughts unceasingly; then shall thy confidence wax strong in the presence of

---

8: Gordon B. Hinckley, "A Tragic Evil among Us," Ensign, Nov. 2004, 61.
9: Jeffrey R. Holland, "Of Souls, Symbols, and Sacraments," BYU Devotional, January 12, 1988

God; and the doctrine of the priesthood shall distil upon thy soul as the dews from heaven. The Holy Ghost shall be thy constant companion."[10]

Those who succeed in overcoming inappropriate thoughts and behaviors are those who learn to engage in virtuous daily routines. So how does one maintain virtuous thoughts unceasingly? Virtuous thoughts may be maintained by doing the following suggestions:

⬥ Listening to uplifting music.

⬥ Enjoying God's creations in nature.

⬥ Keeping our bodies clean and healthy.

⬥ Reading the scriptures and good literature.

⬥ Delighting in laughter with good friends and family.

⬥ Participating in conversation that is not demeaning or lewd.

⬥ Giving thanks in prayer and pleading for power to resist temptation.

⬥ Surrounding ourselves with virtuous things in our homes and workplaces, including pictures, paintings, gifts from loved ones, items that make us laugh, or things that help us recall meaningful memories.

All of these activities can become symbols of virtue, which can keep our minds focused and less susceptible to the cravings of the natural man. If youth can learn and implement these strategies in their lives, they will begin to experience the incredible blessings spoken of in Doctrine and Covenants 121.

It is also vital that they understand we all have weakness to overcome. Weakness does not make us unworthy of God's love. In fact, overcoming our weakness is part of the Lord's plan for us. When the Lord makes us aware of our weakness and we follow His directive to become humble and submissive (not distressed and hopeless), wonderful things begin to happen. We can yield our hearts to the Lord in faith. Then, through His grace and power—not through our willpower alone—He will "make weak things become strong unto us."[11]

We are not told that He will take our weakness away from us. We may continue to be tempted and troubled by our weakness, but as we are humble and maintain faith, the Lord will help us resist temptations.

When young people have problems with pornography, they need to know that they are not lost, that we and the Lord still love them, and that there is a way out. President Hinckley has said: "May you plead with the Lord out of the depths of your soul that He will remove from you the addiction which enslaves you. And may you have the courage to seek the loving guidance of your bishop and, if necessary, the counsel of caring professionals."[12]. Our youth should not feel ashamed of seeking parental, priesthood, and professional help.

Be an Involved Parent or Leader

As parents and leaders, we must be involved in our youths' lives, striving to create a safe environment for them. We need to be bold in our communication with them about these important issues, encouraging them to stay close to the principles of the gospel and to fortify themselves against the powers of the adversary. We need to be aware of and monitor our youths' activities—including their Internet use—and openly discuss the blessings and dangers of human sexuality, listening and giving sound direction and guidance.

Of course, we do not share personal accounts of our own intimate experiences. But using the principles discussed in this article, we can help our youth clearly understand the power and the potential of the sexual urges they have.

More important, we must set an example to our youth. They are watching how we cope with negative influences. Our youth need to know that we know the influence of the adversary is no match for the divine power and influence of the Lord, in whom we place our complete, unwavering confidence.

Section

6

10: *D&C 121:45–46*

11: *Ether 12:27*

12: *Gordon B. Hinckley, "A Tragic Evil Among Us," Ensign, Nov. 2004, 62*

Additional Information for Overcoming Pornography

Let Virtue Garnish Thy Thoughts is a new pamphlet published by the LDS Church designed to help those struggling with pornography. It discusses how to:

◆ Recognize destructive media

◆ Resist and avoid the temptation of pornography

◆ Abandon pornography addictions

Creating a Safe Place to Talk About Dangerous Things

Jeffrey J. Ford, MS, LMFT (Licensed Marriage and Family Therapist)

Sex and pornography have become a top priority for parents and their children to discuss in recent years. With research indicating that adolescents today appear to be using pornography much more than any other age group,[13] parents need to know how to talk about

pornography and how to recognize signs that their child may be already struggling with pornography. In a study conducted at Brigham Young University by Jason Carroll (2008) and others,[14] it was found that 9 out of 10 boys and one third of girls use pornography. Research like this can be sobering and overwhelming for parents today. Talking about pornography and sex is particularly difficult for parents who didn't have that type of discussion with their parents when they were children. Some parents are unsure or confused about when to talk to their children about such an important topic and feel torn between giving their child too much information or too little for their age. In whatever situation parents find themselves, it is helpful to remember that it is never too late to change and make things right.

The first thing that parents have to realize as they begin having this conversation is that this is not a one-time "talk" that will occur in an evening or at dinner. Many people have described their experience of having a one-time "talk" with their parents. One young man shared that his father took him on a long walk

---

13: Arnett, J. J. (2006). *"Emerging Adulthood: Understanding the New Way of Coming of Age."* In J. J. Arnett & J. L. Tanner (Eds.), Emerging adults in America: Coming of Age in the 21st Century *(pp. 3–20).* Washington, D.C.: American Psychological Association.

14: Carolyn McNamara Barry and Stephanie D. Madsen Jason S. Carroll, Laura M. Padilla-Walker, Larry J. Nelson, Chad D. Olson *"Generation XXX: Pornography Acceptance and Use Among Emerging Adults."* Journal of Adolescent Research *2008; 23; 6*

when he was twelve years old and that when the walk ended he never heard anything about sex or pornography again. He told me, "I was in shock! My dad talked for two hours about things I had never heard of before." The result was that the boy took all of the confusing information his father gave him and did two things: (1) He asked his friends about it; he shared that this confused him even more because it was clear that many of his friends were as ignorant as he was; (2) He went to the Internet and looked things up. This boy's World Wide Web inquiry began innocently enough, but that day it ended in an exposure to pornography that created a hunger that developed into a full-fledged addiction. Repeatedly having this discussion with your son or daughter provides an opportunity for them to sort through confusing information and experiences, and it also ensures that the parent is the person who gives the most accurate, safe information.

It is also helpful to remember that an adolescent will open up about things in stages and rarely discloses something all at once. Teenagers are trying to make sense of what is going on around them, what their peers are doing, and whether they will be accepted. Sometimes parents scare their children away when they are approached with one question. Parents become so eager to help that they might think, "At last, a chance to unload!" As the parent unloads everything, the child will likely tune out and feel lectured, and most importantly, his or her needs will not be met. It is helpful to remember that our children will not learn everything at once, and we don't need cover everything at once either. Learning about sex and pornography is a process that takes time and requires safety in asking questions. There isn't one right way to discuss this topic as long as the discussions take place—find a framework or analogy or another way to talk about this that fits for you and draws upon values that are important to you and your family.

Parents must have many conversations about pornography which provide an opportunity to clarify values and beliefs, express opinions, instill truths about sexuality, and answer questions that their child will have. Jill C. Manning, PhD has said parents need to "start having new kinds of conversations about pornography—ones that go beyond scary statistics, frightening forecasts, graphic details and dire realities, and which shift into dialogues that are empowering, hopeful and arm people with practical strategies for being able to address this issue in their own [lives] effectively." These types of conversations go well beyond why pornography is bad and explore what the child thinks and feels about pornography, especially if they have been exposed to pornography already. In essence parents need to create a safe place for their children to talk about dangerous things such as pornography.

Here are some tips that can help parents create safety for their kids as they talk about dangerous things:

1. One way to begin fostering an environment of safety is to stay calm when your son or daughter begins to ask questions about sex or pornography or share their experience with sex or pornography. Teenagers are attuned to their parents' non-verbal cues and will avoid talking about things or asking questions if they sense that Mom or Dad is anxious or upset. Staying calm is particularly important if parents discover that their teenager has been looking at pornography. In this case, parents should carefully plan a response that is based on understanding and helping their teen instead of punishing or shaming them.

   One of the most important things a parent can do is to ask questions such as "How long have you been viewing pornography?" or "Have you also masturbated while you looked at pornography?"

   If your teen has been viewing pornography for a significant amount of time, he needs help. If parents can provide a safe place for teens to share their struggle, they will be more likely to come out of hiding.

   One teen I worked with said this: "When my parents caught me looking at porn, it was an answer to prayer! The night before I prayed that something would happen so I could stop looking at porn. I have tried and tried to stop by myself, and I just couldn't do it. I was relieved when my parents found out!" In this case, the parents and teen are more likely to get the help they need to begin recovery.

Another teen shared this: "The last people I want to tell are my parents! Whenever the subject of pornography comes up, my parents talk about how sick and wrong people are who look at it! Well, I look at it, so they will not love me if I tell them."

The way parents talk about people who look at pornography will contribute to creating a safe place a hostile place for their children. Showing your son or daughter that what they share with you isn't going to send you over the emotional edge creates a lot of safety and encourages them to share more.

2. It is also important that parents create room to make mistakes along the way as teens begin recovery. Telling your child "Don't ever let me catch you looking at pornography again" may cause a lot of panic, especially if the teenager has already attempted to stop and failed.

One young man shared that after his parents caught him, they scolded him and forbade him to ever do it again. He said, "My parents didn't understand! I had already tried to stop and I couldn't do it. How do they expect me to just turn it off? So I just stopped talking about it with them, because I didn't want to disappoint them anymore."

Teenagers need a safe place to talk about how a slip affects them and how to do better the next time. Inviting your child to come to you whenever he is struggling opens the door and prevents him from going underground with his addiction.

3. Many parents also get caught in the trap of offering false forgiveness when their teen begins the disclosure process. False forgiveness usually occurs soon after an adolescent discloses something to their parent and the parent says

something to this effect: "It doesn't matter, it's water under the bridge, I forgive you and I love you, and I've always loved you!"

Certainly, communicating love when your child has done something wrong is important; however, *love* is not *forgiveness*. Forgiveness can only occur when everything that was done has been disclosed, and each person has had time to sort out how they feel about it. Remember, much of the time initial disclosure begins the process of getting the whole story, and is rarely the whole story!

Offering forgiveness will most likely feel cheap and fake to someone who knows that there is more, and it does nothing to provide safety. It also devalues the learning process for the adolescent to be accountable for what they have done. The bottom line is to remember that forgiveness is a process just like disclosure, and reminding your son that you are committed to work with them will create a lot of safety. It is generally more helpful for a parent to commit to being there for their child and helping them in any way possible to overcome their addiction to pornography.

The most important thing to keep in mind as parents talk with their teens about pornography is that together they can find solutions. Pornography's influence diminishes when a teen has a safe place to talk about it. In cases when a child has become addicted, it is important to maintain a safe place where your child can come back for healing and support as he struggles. Creating a safe place will positively influence your child's belief that he can overcome his addiction.

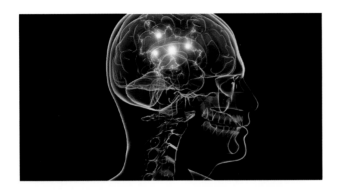

Can Pornography Use Become an Actual Brain Addiction?

Donald L. Hilton, Jr., MD, FACS

Clinical Associate Professor, Department of Neurosurgery
University of Texas Health Sciences Center at San Antonio

The human brain is programmed to incentivize behaviors that contribute to survival. The mesolimbic dopaminergic system rewards eating and sexuality with powerful pleasure incentives. Cocaine, opioids, alcohol, and other drugs subvert, or hijack, these pleasure systems and cause the brain to think a drug high is necessary to survive. There is now strong evidence that natural rewards such as food and sex affect the reward systems in the same way drugs affect them, thus explaining the current interest in "natural addiction." Addiction, whether to cocaine, food, or sex, occurs when the drug use, eating, or sexual behavior ceases to contribute to a state of homeostasis and instead causes adverse consequences. For instance, when eating causes morbid obesity in an organism, few will argue that the organism is in healthy balance. Similarly, pornography causes harm when it impairs or destroys a person's ability to develop emotional intimacy.

A decade ago, evidence began to point to the addictive nature of over-consumption of natural behaviors which cause a dopaminergic reward in the brain. For instance, Dr. Howard Shaffer, Director of Addiction Research at Harvard University, said in 2001, "I had great difficulty with my own colleagues when I suggested that a lot of addiction is the result of experience... repetitive, high-emotion, high-frequency experience. But it has become clear that neuroadaptation—that is, changes in neural circuitry that help perpetuate the behavior—occurs even in the absence of drug-taking."[15] In the decade since he said this, Dr. Shaffer has focused his research more and more on the brain effects of natural addictions, such as gambling.

The experts are fond of saying that addiction occurs when a habit "hijacks" brain circuits that evolved to reward survival, enhancing behaviors such as eating and sex. "It stands to reason if you can derange these circuits with pharmacology, you can do it with natural rewards too," observes Stanford University psychologist Brian Knutson. Thus, drugs are no longer at the heart of the matter. "What is coming up fast as being the central core issue... is continued engagement in self-destructive behavior despite adverse consequences," says Steven Grant of the National Institute on Drug Abuse.[16]

In the decade since these revolutionary concepts were first described, the evidence for the natural reward addiction concept has only become stronger. In 2005, Dr. Eric Nestler, now chairman of neuroscience at Mount Sinai Medical Center in New York, published a landmark paper in Nature Neuroscience titled "Is There a Common Pathway for Addiction?" He said:

Growing evidence indicates that the VTA-NAc pathway and the other limbic regions cited above similarly mediate, at least in part, the acute positive emotional effects of natural rewards, such as food, sex and social interactions. These same regions have also been implicated in the so-called 'natural addictions' (that is, compulsive consumption of natural rewards) such as pathological overeating, pathological gambling and sexual addictions. Preliminary findings suggest that shared pathways may be involved: [an example is] cross-sensitization that occurs between natural rewards and drugs of abuse.[17]

In 2002, a study on cocaine addiction was published which demonstrated measurable volume loss in several areas of the brain, including the frontal lobes, as a result

15: Constance Holden, "Behavioral Addictions: Do They Exist?" Science, 294 (5544) 2 Nov. 2001, pg. 980.

16: Ibid.

17: Eric J. Nestler, "Is there a common molecular pathway for addiction?" Nature Neuroscience 9(11):1445-9, Nov. 2005

Section 6

of the addiction.[18] The technique used was an MRI-based protocol called voxel-based morphometry (VBM), where one-millimeter cubes of brain tissue are quantified and compared. Another VBM study was published in 2004 on methamphetamine with very similar findings.[19] While interesting, these findings are not surprising to either the scientist or the layperson, since cocaine and methamphetamine are "real drugs."

The story becomes more interesting when we look at a natural addiction, such as overeating leading to obesity. In 2006 a VBM study was published looking specifically at obesity, and the results were very similar to the cocaine and methamphetamine studies.[20] The obesity study demonstrated multiple areas of brain volume loss, particularly in the frontal lobes, areas associated with judgment and control. While this study is significant in demonstrating visible damage in a natural endogenous addiction, as opposed to an exogenous drug addiction, it is still easier to accept intuitively because we can see the effects of overeating in the obese person.

So what about sexual addiction? In 2007, a VBM study out of Germany looked specifically at pedophilia and demonstrated almost identical finding to the cocaine, methamphetamine, and obesity studies.[21] This study demonstrates that a sexual compulsion can cause physical, anatomic change, that is, harm, in the brain. Interestingly, a recent paper found a high correlation between pedophilic pornography and sexually abusing children.[22] This noted, the paper thus focused on a subgroup of people with severe pornography addiction, among other problems. While we may draw ethical and legal distinctions between child and adult pornography, the brain is not likely to have such an age-related set point with regard to dopaminergic downgrading and addiction-based volume loss. Does the brain care whether the person is physically experiencing sexuality, or doing it through the medium of object sex, for example, pornography? The mirror systems of the brain turn the virtual experience of pornography into a real experience, as far as the brain is concerned. This is supported by a recent study from France showing activation of areas associated with mirror neurons in

18: Teresa R. Franklin, Paul D. Acton, Joseph A Maldjian, Jason D. Gray, Jason R. Croft, Charles A. Dackis, Charles P. O'Brien, and Anna Rose Childress, "Decreased Gray Matter Concentration in the Insular, Orbitofrontal, Cingulate, and Temporal Cortices of Cocaine Patients," Biological Psychiatry (51)2, January 15, 2002, 134-142.

19: Paul M. Thompson, Kikralee M. Hayashi, Sara L. Simon, Jennifer A. Geaga, Michael S. Hong, Yihong Sui, Jessica Y. Lee, Arthur W. Toga, Walter Ling, and Edythe D. London, "Structural Abnormalities in the Brains of Human Subjects Who Use Methamphetamine," The Journal of Neuroscience, 24(26) June 30 2004;6028-6036.

20: Nicola Pannacciulli, Angelo Del Parigi, Kewei Chen, Dec Son N.T. Le, Eric M. Reiman and Pietro A. Tataranni, "Brain abnormalities in human obesity: A voxel-based morphometry study." Neuroimage 31(4) July 15 2006, 1419-1425.

21: Boris Schiffer, Thomas Peschel, Thomas Paul, Elke Gizewski, Michael Forshing, Norbert Leygraf, Manfred Schedlowske, and Tillmann H.C. Krueger, "Structural Brain Abnormalities in the Frontostriatal System and Cerebellum in Pedophilia," Journal of Psychiatric Research (41)9, November 2007, 754-762.

22: M. Bourke, A. Hernandez, The 'Butner Study' Redux: A Report of the Incidence of Hands-on Child Victimization by Child Pornography Offenders. Journal of Family Violence 24(3) 2009, 183-191.

the brain of human males viewing pornography. The authors conclude that "the mirror-neuron system prompts the observers to resonate with the motivational state of other individuals appearing in visual depictions of sexual interactions."[23] A preliminary study supports frontal brain damage specifically in patients unable to control their sexual behavior.[24] This study used diffusion MRI to evaluate function of nerve transmission through white matter, where the axons, or wires connecting nerve cells, are located. It demonstrated dysfunction in the superior frontal region, an area associated with compulsivity, a hallmark of addiction.

Also pertinent is a paper from the Mayo Clinic on treatment of Internet pornography addiction with naltrexone, an opioid receptor antagonist.[25] Drs. Bostsick and Bucci at Mayo Clinic treated a patient with the inability to control his Internet pornography use.

The patient was placed on naltrexone, a drug which acts on the opioid system to decrease dopamine's ability to stimulate cells in the nucleus accumbens. With this drug, he was able to obtain control of his sexual life. The authors conclude:

"In summary, cellular adaptations in the addict's PFC result in increased salience of drug-associated stimuli, decreased salience of non-drug stimuli, and decreased interest in pursuing goal-directed activities central to survival. In addition to naltrexone's approval from the Food and Drug Administration for treating alcoholism, several published case reports have demonstrated its potential for treating pathologic gambling, self-injury, kleptomania, and compulsive sexual behavior. We believe this is the first description of its use to combat Internet sexual addiction."

The prestigious Royal Society of London was founded in the 1660s, and publishes the longest running scientific journal in the world. In a recent issue of the Philosophical Transactions of the Royal Society, the current state of the understanding of addiction was reported as discussed by some of the world's leading addiction scientists at a Society meeting. The title of the journal issue reporting the meeting was "The Neurobiology of Addiction—New Vistas." Interestingly, of the 17 articles, two were specifically concerned with natural addiction: one was on pathologic gambling[26] and the other was a paper by Dr. Nora Volkow on similarities in brain dysfunction in drug addiction and in overeating.[27] A third paper by Dr. Nestler addressed animal models of natural addiction as well with regard to DeltaFosB.[28]

DeltaFosB is a chemical which Dr. Nestler has studied, and appears to be found in the neurons of addicted subjects. It appears to have a physiologic role as well, but is strongly implicated in addiction. Interestingly, it was first found in the brain cells of animals studied in drug addiction, but has now been found in brain cells in the nucleus accumbens related to over-consumption of natural rewards. A recent paper investigating DeltaFosB and its role in over-consumption of two natural rewards, eating and sexuality, concludes:

"In summary, the work presented here provides evidence that, in addition to drugs of abuse, natural rewards induce DeltaFosB levels in the Nac… our results raise the possibility that DeltaFosB induction in the Nac may mediate not only key aspects of drug addiction, but also aspects of so-called natural addictions involving compulsive consumption of natural rewards."[29]

Dr. Nora Volkow is head of the National Institute on Drug Abuse (NIDA), and is one of the most published and respected addiction scientists in the world. She has

Section

6

23: H. Mouras, S. Stoleru, V. Moulier, M Pelegrini-Issac, R. Rouxel, B Grandjean, D. Glutron, J Bittoun, Activation of mirror-neuron system by erotic video clips predicts degree of induced erection: an fMRI study. NeuroImage 42 (2008) 1142-1150.

24: Michael H. Miner, Nancy Raymond, Bryon A. Meuller, Martin Lloyd, Kelvin Ol Lim, "Preliminary investigation of the impulsive and neuroanatomical characteristics of compulsive sexual behavior." Psychiatry Research Neuroimaging volume 174, issue 2, November 30 2009, pages 146-151.

25: J. Michael Bostwick and Jeffrey A. Bucci, "Internet Sex Addiction Treated With Naltrexone." Mayo Clinic Proceedings, 2008, 83(2):226-230.

26: Marc N. Potenza, "The neurobiology of pathologic gambling and drug addiction: an overview and new findings," Philosophical Transactions of the Royal Society, 363, 2008, 3181-3190.

27: Nora D. Volkow, Gene-Jack Wang, Joanna S. Fowler, Frank Telang, "Overlapping neuronal circuits in addiction and obesity: evidence of systems pathology," Philosophical Transactions of the Royal Society, 363, 2008, 3191-3200.

28: Eric J. Nestler, "Transcriptional mechanisms of addiction: role of DeltaFosB," Philosophical Transactions of the Royal Society, 363, 2008, 3245-3256.

29: D.L. Wallace, et al, The Influence of DeltaFosB in the Nucleus Accumberns on Natural reward-Related Behavior, The Journal of Neuroscience, 28(4): October 8, 2008, 10272-10277.

recognized this evolution in the understanding of natural addiction and has advocated changing the name of the NIDA to the National Institute on Diseases of Addiction. The journal *Science* reports: "NIDA director Nora Volkow also felt that her institute's name should encompass addictions such as pornography, gambling, and food,". . . "She would like to send the message that [we should] look at the whole field"[30]

In summary, in the last 10 years the evidence has become firmly supportive of the addictive nature of natural rewards. Drs. Malenka and Kauer, in their landmark paper on the mechanism of the chemical changes which occur in the brain cells of addicted individuals, state, "Addiction represents a pathological, yet powerful form of learning and memory."[31] We now call these changes in brain cells "long-term potentiation" and "long-term depression," and speak of the brain as being plastic, or subject to change and rewire. Dr. Norman Doidge, a neurologist at Columbia, in his book *The Brain That Changes Itself,* describes how pornography causes a rewiring of the neural circuits. He notes a study on men as they viewed Internet pornography in which the men looked "uncannily" like rats pushing the lever to receive cocaine in the

experimental Skinner boxes. Like the addicted rat, they were desperately seeking the next fix, clicking the mouse—just like the rat pushed the lever. Pornography addiction is frantic learning, and perhaps this is why many who have struggled with multiple addictions report that it was the hardest addiction for them to overcome. *Drug* addictions, while powerful, are more passive in a "thinking" kind of way, whereas *pornography* viewing—especially on the Internet—is a much more active process neurologically. The constant searching and evaluation of each image or video clip, which have been carefully produced for potency and effect, is an exercise in neuronal learning and rewiring.

In August of 2011 the American Society of Addiction Medicine (ASAM) formally recognized destructive compulsive consumption of natural rewards, including food, sex, and gambling, as natural addictions. The new definition makes two bold statements. First, addiction is a disease of the brain. Second, addiction is not limited to substances such as cocaine and opioids, but includes behaviors involving food, sex, and gambling. Consider this excerpt from the definition:

Addiction is a primary, chronic disease of brain reward, motivation, memory and related circuitry. Addiction affects neurotransmission and interactions within reward structures of the brain, including the

---

30: Science *6 July 2007: ol. 317. no. 5834, p. 2 (emphasis added).*
31: *Julie A. Kauer, Robert C. Malenka, "Synaptic Plasticity and Addiction," Nature Reviews Neuroscience, 8, 8440858 November 2007, 844-858.*

nucleus accumbens, anterior cingulate cortex, basal forebrain and amygdala, such that motivational hierarchies are altered and addictive behaviors, which may or may not include alcohol and other drug use, supplant healthy, self-care related behaviors. Addiction also affects neurotransmission and interactions between cortical and hippocampal circuits and brain reward structures, such that the memory of previous exposures to rewards (such as food, sex, alcohol and other drugs) leads to a biological and behavioral response to external cues, in turn triggering craving and/or engagement in addictive behaviors.[32]

The definition is unambiguous and direct, and affirms the primary role neurobiology plays in all addictions. The definition was four years in the making and involved over 80 addiction experts. With regard to biology, it is definitive and therefore describes compulsive destructive sexual behavior as a brain addiction. Some clarifications from ASAM about sexual addiction are found on their site under the heading "Frequently asked questions," as follows:

QUESTION: This new definition of addiction refers to addiction involving gambling, food, and sexual behaviors. Does ASAM really believe that food and sex are addicting?

Answer: Addiction to gambling has been well described in the scientific literature for several decades. In fact, the latest edition of the DSM (DSM-V) will list gambling disorder in the same section with substance use disorders.

The new ASAM definition makes a departure from equating addiction with just substance dependence, by describing how addiction is also related to behaviors that are rewarding. This the first time that ASAM has taken an official position that addiction is not solely "substance dependence." This definition says that addiction is about functioning and brain circuitry and how the structure and function of the brains of persons with addiction differ from the structure and function of the brains of persons who do not have addiction. It talks about reward

circuitry in the brain and related circuitry, but the emphasis is not on the external rewards that act on the reward system. Food and sexual behaviors and gambling behaviors can be associated with the "pathological pursuit of rewards" described in this new definition of addiction.

QUESTION: Who has food addiction or sex addiction?

Answer: We all have the brain reward circuitry that makes food and sex rewarding. In fact, this is a survival mechanism. In a healthy brain, these rewards have feedback mechanisms for satiety or 'enough.' In someone with addiction, the circuitry becomes dysfunctional such that the message to the individual becomes 'more', which leads to the pathological pursuit of rewards and/or relief through the use of substances and behaviors. So, anyone who has addiction is vulnerable to food and sex addiction.

We do not have accurate figures for how many people are affected by food addiction or sex addiction, specifically. We believe it would be important to focus research on gathering this information by recognizing these aspects of addiction, which may be present with or without substance-related problems.[33]

Understanding these concepts will allow those who struggle with pornography and other sexual addictions to give the necessary effort to obtain sobriety. It will also help family members understand why it is so difficult for their loved one to gain healing.

Human sexual climax utilizes the same reward pathways as those mobilized during a heroin rush.[34] If we fail to understand the implications of pornography's ability to re-program the brain structurally, neurochemically, and metabolically, we doom ourselves to continue to fail in treating this formidable disease. However, if we accord this powerful natural reward the appropriate focus and emphasis, we can help many who are now trapped in addiction and despair, to find peace and hope.

32: ASAM definition, long version
http://www.asam.org/DefinitionofAddiction-LongVersion.html

33: Frequently Asked Questions/ ASAM definition.
http://www.asam.org/pdf/Advocacy/20110816_DefofAddiction-FAQs.pdf
34: Gert Holstege, Janniko R. Georgiadis, Anne M.J. Paans, Linda C. Meiners, Ferdinand H.C. E. van der Graaf, and A.A.T. Simone Reinders, " Brain activation during human male ejaculation," The Journal of Neuroscience 23 (27), 2003, 9185-9193

Section 6

APPROPRIATELY DISCUSSING AND TEACHING *about the topic of pornography in the home can be a challenge. To assist parents in this process, the following sample lesson plans have been prepared. The lessons can be given in their entirety or they can be presented in sections. For example, a parent teaching a family home evening lesson may choose to address only one section each week from "Children: Our Bodies Are Special Gifts." Lessons should be adapted for age, maturity, and prior understanding. Parents who teach about or discuss the topic of pornography should carefully study the lessons and other material in this manual and then decide what their children most need to hear.*

Sample lessons in this manual:

- **Sample Lesson A:** Our Bodies Are Special Gifts (for Children) . . . . Pg 108

- **Sample Lesson B:** Teaching about Pornography (for Teenagers) . . . . Pg 113

- **Sample Lesson C:** Discussing Pornography (for Teenagers) . . . . Pg 117

- **Sample Lesson D:** Developing Christlike Relationships That Lead to Marriage (for Young Single Adults) . . . . Pg 122

- **Sample Lesson E:** Replacing Fear with Faith (for General Audience) . . . . Pg 127

Section

7

Sample Lesson A: Our Bodies Are Special Gifts

A Resource Lesson Guide for Teaching Young Children about Healthy Sexuality and Pornography

◈ **Audience:** Children ages 4–11

◈ **Purpose:** To aid parents in teaching young children about our bodies, healthy sexuality, and pornography in the home

◈ **Outline:** (1) Introduction, (2) We Are Special, (3) The Importance of Gender, (4) Pornography, (5) Our Divine Potential, and (6) Conclusion

Suggested Preparation

Carefully read the lesson and pray about what you should present. Review "Discussion Points for Children" in the Discussion Points section of this book. Find a family heirloom to use as part of your presentation. Set aside a chalkboard and chalk, or something else on which to write. Read *"The Family: A Proclamation to the World"* and list information about male/female gender roles on 3x5 cards. Prepare yourself to discuss questions regarding the body and sexuality. Gather winter clothing. Print off the "Family Pledge" for all members of the family to sign.

Introduction

After teaching this or similar lessons, you may wish to speak with each child individually and get a better feel for their level of exposure to pornography and the help that may be needed. This lesson should be adapted to the age, maturity, and prior understanding of your children. Sections may be divided into separate lessons. Depending on the age and maturity of the children, a 5–10 minute lesson format might be best.

We Are Special

Suggested Activity

Begin by showing a treasured object in your home, such as a family heirloom, that you and your children value. Explain, or have the children explain, why the object is precious and how sad you would feel if it were broken.

Q: How do we take care of special things?

A: Protect them and treat them with respect.

Q: What is the most special thing in this room?

A: We are!

Q: Why are we so special?

A: We are unique children of our Heavenly Parents.

Q: What is our spirit?

A: The part of us we cannot see.

Q: How do we take care of our spirit?

A: Learn and apply the teachings of Jesus Christ and follow the promptings of the Holy Ghost.

Q: What do we do to take care of our body?

A: Follow the Word of Wisdom, treat our bodies with respect, and dress modestly.

Suggested Activity

You may consider having your children list specific ways in which they can exhibit modesty and take care of their spirits and bodies.

The Importance of Gender

Suggested Activity

Create two headings, male and female. Before the lesson, read *"The Family: A Proclamation to the World"* and write on separate 3x5 cards specific information about each gender role. Put the 3x5 cards face down on the ground. Give each child an opportunity to select a card and decide under which heading it would go: male or female. Consider reading sections of the Proclamation. Below are possible elements for 3x5 cards:

⬧ **Male**: husband; father; presides over family; provides food, water, and home; protects family; teaches children to follow God; teaches children to love and serve; helps wife.

⬧ **Female**: mother; wife; gives birth; feeds children; educates and trains, supports and encourages children; teaches children to follow God; teaches children to love and serve; helps husband.

Q: When was it decided that we would be a boy or girl?

A: When we were born as spirits to our Heavenly Parents.

Section 7

Q: What is gender and why is it important?

A: Our gender is what we call being either "boy" or "girl." Being boy or girl is important because it is part of our divine nature, destiny, purpose, and identity.[1]

Q: What makes boys different from girls?

A: Being a boy or a girl is an important part of who we are.[2] Boys and girls have unique roles and purposes in God's plan. Boys and girls are also born with unique bodies. Our bodies have special purposes based on our gender and should be kept sacred. We all have questions about the body and we do not need to be embarrassed or afraid to ask questions. It is good to learn about our bodies. When we have questions about our bodies or the purpose of different parts, it is important to talk to our parents. If we ask friends, they may not fully understand important concepts, or they may talk about the body in a way that is disrespectful. When we ask parents, they can help us to understand the true purpose of our bodies.

Suggested Activity

Based on the child's own pace and comfort level, teach basic concepts regarding sexuality, body parts, and body functions.[3] Ask children if they have questions. Let these questions guide your discussion. Be prepared to answer questions simply, honestly, and accurately. This requires parents to be prepared to know the names of body parts and at least basic facts about body functions. Many excellent resources exist for teaching young children these concepts, including *A Parent's Guide* published by the LDS Church. Parents should consider having several lessons or discussions over time on this topic, depending on the changing maturity of the child.

1: *The Family: A Proclamation to the World, available at www.lds.org/family/proclamation?lang=eng.*

2: *Ibid.*

3: *A Parent's Guide, chapter 4, available at www.lds.org/ldsorg/v/index.jsp hideNav=1&locale=0&sourceId=be637befabc20110VgnVCM100000176f620a___&vgnextoid=198bf4b13819d110VgnVCM1000003a94610aRCRD.*

Pornography

Our bodies are gifts that are special and sacred. Everyone who is born to earth gets a body. Since Satan does not have a body, he tries to make us mistreat our bodies so we are unhappy. One way that Satan does this is through pornography.

Suggested Activity

Ask your children if they have ever seen pictures in the mall, on the Internet, on TV, or in other places that show people who are not dressed modestly or are not showing respect for their bodies. Ask them how they feel when they see these pictures. Explain that many of these types of pictures and videos are pornography. Gauge the level of exposure, understanding of sexual issues, and a child's readiness to discuss these topics in more detail based on each child's response. It is important to realize that some children could have minimal exposure, while others may have had repeated exposure to pornography.

Q: What is pornography?

A: Satan would have us look at pictures and videos of people who dress immodestly, show their naked bodies, or make fun of proper intimacy. We call these kinds of dirty pictures, stories, and videos "pornography." (As the child matures, the discussion broadens to explain that pornography is material designed to arouse sexual feelings in people and can include photos, films, music, and books.[4])

4: *Jill C. Manning, PhD,* What's the Big Deal about Pornography?, *p 3.*

Q: Can you name some places pornography is found?

A: Television, radio, books, movies, photographs, magazines, DVDs, CDs, cell phones, iPods, video games, websites, webcams, live performances, and the shopping mall. It is very common to find pornography on computers, and pornography may be found at a friend's house. It is important to tell friends who have these pictures or videos that you don't want to look at that kind of stuff, and then leave. Make sure to talk to your mom or dad about what happened.

Q: Why is pornography bad?

A: Pornography is bad because our bodies are sacred and should be treated with respect. It can cause feelings of guilt and shame that lead us to lie and hide these pictures and videos. Viewing pornography can interfere with our ability to feel the Spirit and follow God. It can weaken our ability to make correct choices because pornography is addictive, just like other drugs. Addiction is when we engage in certain actions that hurt us and it becomes really hard to stop; we feel like we can't stop, —even when we want to.

Suggested Activity

Gather a snow hat, gloves, scarf, coat, and umbrella. Dress a child with the articles while discussing the dangers of being caught in a storm. Demonstrate the effectiveness of these articles in protecting us. Talk about what kind of shelter would provide protection in a storm. Explain to your children that protecting ourselves from pornography is every bit as important as protecting ourselves from a storm. President Hinckley said, "The excuse is given that [pornography] is hard to avoid, that it is right at our fingertips, and that there is no escape. Suppose a storm is raging and the winds howl and snow swirls about you. You find yourself unable to stop it. But you can dress properly and seek shelter, [so] the storm will have no effect on you."[5]

Q: What should I do if I see pornography?

A: When most children see pornography, they want to hide it because they are ashamed or embarrassed and do not know what to do. Whenever you see pornography, think "That is pornography!" and quickly cover your eyes and turn away. Then go to your parents as soon as possible and tell them about it. If you find a picture, magazine, or Internet site that makes you curious about the body, show it to your parents. Ask your parents any questions you might have. If you hear a conversation or something that makes you have questions, ask your parents. Your parents can help you to understand more about what you are seeing and hearing, and they can help you understand any feelings you might have. There are no bad questions. You can ask your parents anything you are curious about.

Suggested Activity

Have your children role-play regarding how they would react if they saw pornography at a friend's house, the mall, on a cell phone, or in another situation.

Q: How can I avoid pornography?

A: Heavenly Father can help us to avoid pornography and other negative things when we pray for help. It is important for us to be careful about what we do with our friends. If a friend offers to show you a picture, magazine, or Internet site that you think is pornography or makes you feel uncomfortable, tell them no. If they are talking about the body in a way that makes you uncomfortable or is not respectful, ask them to stop and then tell your parents. Always talk about the body with respect. Only go places on the Internet that your parents say are okay and only use the Internet when you are with adults. It is important for all of us to dress modestly and treat our bodies with respect. It is also important for all of us to only watch and listen to good shows, movies, and music.

Section 7

5: President Gordon B. Hinckley, *A Tragic Evil Among Us*, Ensign, *Nov. 2005, 61.*

Suggested Activity

Discuss what media is appropriate in your home and set specific standards. Consider creating a family pledge that is signed by all members and posted in a public place, perhaps by the computer or television.[6]

Our Divine Potential

Help children to understand that they have inherited divine qualities from Heavenly Father. We are His children. As we try to choose the right every day, Heavenly Father will help us resist temptations and do good things. Eventually, we can return to live with Him. Consider sharing the following story. The story of Joseph in Egypt could also be used.

Many years ago I heard the story of the son of King Louis XVI of France. King Louis had been taken from his throne and imprisoned. His young son, the prince, was taken by those who dethroned the king. They thought that inasmuch as the king's son was heir to the throne, if they could destroy him morally, he would never realize the great and grand destiny that life had bestowed upon him.

They took him to a community far away, and there they exposed the lad to every filthy and vile thing that life could offer. They exposed him to foods the richness of which would quickly make him a slave to appetite. They used vile language around him constantly. They exposed him to lewd and lusting women. They exposed him to dishonor and distrust. He was surrounded 24 hours a day by everything that could drag the soul of a man as low as one could slip. For over six months he had this treatment—but not once did the young lad buckle under pressure. Finally, after intensive temptation, they questioned him. Why had he not submitted himself to these things—why had he not partaken? These things would provide pleasure, satisfy his lusts, and were desirable; they were all his. The boy said, "I cannot do what you ask for I was born to be a king."

— ELDER VAUGHN J. FEATHERSTONE
"The King's Son," *New Era*, November 1975, 35

Help your children understand that they are much like the prince. Our Heavenly Father is a King, and just as the king's son was exposed to every vile thing in this life, sometimes we are exposed to filth and degradation. But we are all born to be kings and queens in the Kingdom of God. We too must be like the boy in the story and remember who we are and what we can become. Unlike the prince, we can avoid and get away from damaging material. We must turn away from evil and always choose the right, even when our friends do not.

Conclusion

We are sent to earth to be happy and learn how to become like God. As we treat our bodies with respect, choose good media, and avoid pornography, we will be blessed. We have parents and a Heavenly Father who love us deeply. As we have questions about these or any other topics, we do not need to be ashamed. We can go to our parents and they will help us find answers.

6: *www.deseretbook.com/mediapledge. See Suggested Books, DVDs, and Other Resources in this manual.*

Sample Lesson B: Teaching about Pornography

A Parent's Resource Lesson Guide for Teaching Teenagers about Healthy Sexuality and Pornography

◈ **Audience:** Youth ages 12–18

◈ **Purpose:** To aid parents in teaching teenagers about pornography in the home

◈ **Outline:** (1) Introduction, (2) About Pornography, (3) Prevention, and (4) Conclusion

Section

7

Suggested Preparation

Carefully read the lesson and pray about what you should present. Read relevant stories from the Personal Stories in the Resources section. Review the handouts in the Resources section.

Introduction

Deceit is "the act or practice of misleading somebody."[7] In Moses 4:1–4 we are taught about Satan's desire to destroy the agency of man. Because of his actions, he and his followers were cast out. Neither Satan nor his followers would ever have the privilege of obtaining

a physical body. Their eternal progression was halted. Is it any wonder Satan's primary aim is to mock the physical body and its divine characteristics? He wants to deceive us and desires our destruction so that we will be miserable like he is. Elder Richard G. Scott has said, "Satan particularly seeks to tempt one who has lived a pure, clean life to experiment through magazines, videos, or movies with powerful images of a woman's or man's body."[8] Elder David A. Bednar has said that "When any of Heavenly Father's children misuse their physical tabernacles by violating the law of chastity, by using drugs and addictive substances, by disfiguring or

7: *Richard G. Scott, "Serious Questions, Serious Answers," Liahona, Sept. 1997*

8: *"Making the Right Choices," Ensign, Nov. 1994 p 37.*

defacing themselves, or by worshipping the false idol of body images, whether their own or that of others, Satan is delighted."[9] A common way Satan tries to tempt and deceive us is through pornography.

About Pornography

Pornography is a problem which is growing increasingly worse. President Hinckley stated that pornography "is like a raging storm, destroying individuals and families, utterly ruining what was once wholesome and beautiful."[10]

Q: What is pornography?

A: Pornography is "material that is sexually explicit and intended primarily for the purpose of sexual arousal."[11] It may depict nudity, sexual behavior, and it may include written materials. It can also be created, distributed, and consumed using any type of media.

Q: What are some of the ways pornography is available?

A: Television, radio, books, movies, photographs, magazines, cartoons, drawings, videos, DVDs, CDs, telephones, cell phones, iPods, video games, websites, web cams, and live performances.

Q: Why is pornography damaging?

A: Did you know that one 30-second commercial spot during the 2008 Super Bowl cost $2.7 million? That is equivalent to $90,000 a second![12] Why would advertisers be willing to pay so much? Because they know if they can position their product in front of people's eyes for even as short a time as 30 seconds, it will create a desire for their product. Visual images create desires; marketers know this—and so does the adversary. What we see affects what we think about, which defines our desires, which precede our actions, which ultimately determines our character. Our

character determines our eternal destiny. Pornography "sells" Satan's lies, lies which teach that there is no connection between sex and honesty, commitment, respect for ourselves and others, and emotional closeness. This lie causes physical addiction, emotional disconnect, social dysfunction, and spiritual death.

Pornography is spiritually destructive. Pornography is extremely disrespectful to the body God has given us and mocks our divine gift of procreation. It conditions viewers to be calloused and crude about these divine gifts. President Hinckley stated:

> *Pornography is poison. Do not watch it or read it. It will destroy you if you do. It will take from you your self-respect. It will rob you of a sense of the beauties of life. It will tear you down and pull you into a slew of evil thoughts and possibly evil actions. Stay away from it. Shun it as you would a foul disease, for it is just as deadly.*
> —PRESIDENT GORDON B. HINCKLEY
> *Ensign,* Nov. 1997

Pornography is addictive and can take control of our lives. Which do you think is more addictive—cocaine or pornography? Elder Oaks has stated:

> *Pornography is addictive. It impairs decision-making capacities and it 'hooks' its users, drawing them back obsessively for more and more. A man who had been addicted to pornography and to hard drugs wrote me this comparison: "In my eyes cocaine doesn't hold a candle to this. I have done both.... Quitting even the hardest drugs was nothing compared to trying to quit pornography."*
> —ELDER DALLIN H. OAKS
> *"Pornography," Ensign,* May 2005

9: *CES Fireside at BYU–Idaho, May 3, 2009.*

10: *Gordon B. Hinckley, "A Tragic Evil Among Us." Ensign, Nov. 2004*

11: *Jill C. Manning, "What's the Big Deal About Pornography?" (2008) Shadow Mountain Press, SLC, UT.*

12: *wiki.answers.com/Q/Cost_of_2008_Super_Bowl_commercial*

Section 7

Scientific data shows sexual arousal stimulated by viewing pornography results in powerful chemical changes in the brain very similar to other substances such as drugs and alcohol. For some, pornography is instantly addictive.

Pornography destroys relationships. Pornography degrades us as children of God and changes the way we view other people. Pornography encourages people to be less sensitive and respectful toward others because it treats people like objects who simply exist to satisfy another person's sexual urges or desires. The act of treating a person like an object is called *objectification*. Objectification takes away human qualities and adds the qualities of an object (something that doesn't speak, doesn't have feelings, and can't make choices) so that people are less likely to relate to, understand, or be sensitive toward the person being shown. When we begin to objectify others, we lose part of our humanity and diminish our divine ability to show empathy and compassion for others.

Pornography negatively affects marriage and can affect our ability to have a normal sexual relationship with our future spouse. Jill C. Manning, PhD, a licensed marriage and family therapist who specializes in research and clinical work related to pornography, states, "Every person I have worked with who has been involved with pornography has had less understanding about relationships and sexuality."[13] Pornography destroys trust, love, and true affection; it cheapens what is special between husband and wife; it decreases desire to marry and have children; and it affects everyone who has contact with the user.

Suggested Activity

Discuss the *Comparing Healthy and Unhealthy Relationships* handout by Jill C. Manning, PhD in the Resources section of this manual.

Prevention

In today's world, it has become almost impossible to avoid pornography completely, but there is still much we can do to limit our exposure and become educated regarding healthy sexuality. Becoming educated regarding healthy sexuality can help us to understand why pornography is bad and how healthy sexuality relates to God's plan. Learn about healthy sexuality. Understanding healthy sexuality is important, given the prevalence of distorted and misleading messages in our society. Parents are here to help you. If you are curious about things you see or hear, talk with your parents. They can help you understand what you are hearing and put things in a proper perspective. There is no question that you need to be embarrassed or ashamed about. They want to help you learn about the body and how it relates to God's plan.

Suggested Activity

Either during the lesson or after, ask teens what questions they have about the body and sexuality. Be prepared with resources to appropriately address questions. See the Resources section of this manual.

What can I do to protect myself? One of Satan's favorite lies is *"One time will not hurt anything."* Our motto needs to be *"Not even once!"* Dr. Manning teaches that if youth "have eyelids that work, a neck

---

13: Jill C. Manning, *"What's the Big Deal About Pornography?"* (2008) Shadow Mountain Press, SLC, UT., p 45

Section

7

that can turn their head, fingers that can push a power button, feet that can walk or run them out of a situation, and a spirit that understands right from wrong, they are qualified to work with parents to keep themselves safe from pornography."[14] If you ever see pornography, protect yourself by (1) saying to yourself that this is pornography, (2) immediately turning off the program, video, or computer, and (3) telling parents immediately. If you think you have a problem with pornography and are having difficulty stopping, talk with your parents or your bishop. They can provide the love, support, and guidance necessary to get help.

What can we do to protect our family? Some families choose to take a careful inventory of media in their homes, prayerfully consider whether any content compromises virtue and then make any necessary corrections. Some families have chosen to create a family pledge supporting their desire for righteous media usage, which each family member signs. The pledge is then placed next to computers, televisions, and so forth in their home as a reminder of their commitment to take a stand for righteousness. Installing Internet filters and exercising Internet safety is also important.

Suggested Activity

As a family, discuss family media standards that all will agree to live by, and write them down. Create a pledge and post it in a public place. Periodically ask in future lessons how family members are doing.

14: Jill C. Manning, (Audio CD) "Let's Talk About the Elephant in the Room," www.deseretbook.com

Conclusion

We can be confident in our ability to overcome the prevalence of pornography in the world around us. We have power to control our sexuality and to protect ourselves from Satan's temptations. With the strength of the Lord, we can overcome any temptation.

President George Albert Smith offered this profound principle and promise:

> *There is a division line well defined that separates the Lord's territory from Lucifer's. If we live on the Lord's side of the line, Lucifer cannot come there to influence us, but if we cross the line into his territory, we are in his power. By keeping the commandments of the Lord we are safe on His side of the line, but if we disobey His teaching we voluntarily cross into the zone of temptation and invite the destruction that is ever present there. Knowing this, how anxious we should always be to live on the Lord's side of the line.*
>
> *We are promised safety, security, and joy as we follow the promptings of the Spirit and practice virtue before the Lord. He will guide and support us in our efforts to be righteous and stay on his side of the line.*
>
> —PRESIDENT GEORGE ALBERT SMITH
> Improvement ERA, May 1935, p 278

Sample Lesson C: Discussing Pornography

Guidelines for Parents Addressing Pornography with Teenagers

* **Audience:** Youth ages 12–18

* **Purpose:** Help youth understand (1) the danger of pornography, (2) the importance of discussing any questions, and (3) the need to disclose pornography exposure with parents and leaders.

* **Outline:** (1) Introduction, (2) Prevention, (3) Recognition, (4) Overcoming, (5) Support, and (6) Conclusion

* **Suggested Preparation:** Carefully read the lesson and pray about what should be presented. Read through "Discussion Points for Teens" in the Discussion section. Read relevant personal stories in the resources section. Review the handouts in the Resource section.

Section

7

Introduction

Suggested Activity

Begin by discussing some of the questions below regarding secrecy:

* Why do little children hide when they have done something wrong?

  * They recognize they have made a mistake and done something that is not right.

* They are ashamed.

* They want to avoid punishment or embarrassment.

* How would a loving parent deal with a little child who has done something wrong and is now hiding?

  * Encourage the child to come out of hiding and resolve the problem.

* Assure the child that they are still loved (replace shame with courage).

* Hold your child accountable for his actions, and teach him how to avoid the mistake in the future and how to repair any damage done.

◆ Why do you think it would be good to disclose behavior you may be ashamed of to a loving parent of leader?

* It helps us to repent of past behaviors and develop new habits and forms of interaction.

* It helps protect us and get us the help we need.

Prevention

Let's now discuss a behavior that frequently causes people to hide in secrecy and shame. That behavior is pornography use. One of the first steps in preventing pornography addiction is to understand pornography and acknowledge that it is always wrong.

Q: What does pornography include?

A: Inappropriate images in books, in magazines, or on the Internet, and inappropriate words or lyrics in books, in songs, in movies, in video games, and in chat rooms. Pornography is material specifically designed to arouse sexual feelings in people. Pornography addiction often leads to inappropriate sexual behavior with oneself

(masturbation) and with others (fornication and adultery).

Q: How big of a problem is pornography?

A: Recently, some research has indicated the following: 30% of unsolicited emails contain pornographic information;[15] the average age of pornography exposure is 11 years old;[16] and 9 out of 10 college age males view pornography at some level, and 31% of college age females view pornography at some level.[17]

Exposure Does Not Equal Addiction

Exposure to pornography is very difficult to avoid. If you accidentally see pornography, immediately label it as pornography, quickly turn away or shut down the website, computer, or magazine, talk with your parents about what occurred, and identify ways pornography could be avoided in the future.

Addiction to pornography differs from *exposure*. Addiction is the inability to stop voluntarily viewing pornography—even when you may want to. Addiction occurs from repeated exposure. If you have quit for a while and then started viewing pornography again, and then quit again and started again, it is likely you are addicted. Addiction to pornography is avoidable and can be prevented by talking to your parents or bishop every time you are exposed to pornography. Pornography addiction requires secrecy and shame to survive.

Recognition

It is important to recognize that pornography is addictive and destroys lives. However, it is also important to realize that addicts can recover with strong desire, a lot of hard work, and time.

Viewing pornography releases a variety of chemicals (drugs) in the body that can physically alter the brain. Pornography addiction is no respecter of persons, and individuals can become addicted at any age. Elder Dallin H. Oaks said this:

15: http://technology.sau16.org/internetsafety/isafe.htm

16: Jerry Roplato, Internet Pornography Statistics, http://internet-filter-review. toptenreviews.com/internet-pornography-statistics.html

17: Journal of Adolescent Research; http://jar.sagepub.com/content/23/1/6.short

Pornography is addictive. It impairs decision-making capacities and it "hooks" its users, drawing them back obsessively for more and more. A man who had been addicted to pornography and to hard drugs wrote me this comparison: "In my eyes cocaine doesn't hold a candle to this. I have done both.... Quitting even the hardest drugs was nothing compared to trying to quit pornography."

—ELDER DALLIN H. OAKS
"Pornography," *Ensign*, May 2005

Q: Why would pornography be harder to quit than drugs?

A: The extended use of pornography causes physical changes in the brain that make it very difficult to stop viewing. The brain center that controls impulsiveness becomes stronger while the center that controls willpower becomes weaker.

Q: How is pornography spiritually damaging?

A: Pornography absolutely mocks and scorns the two most precious gifts our Father in Heaven has given us: our bodies, and the ability to procreate. It also causes an addiction that robs us of our free will. Viewing pornography is so painful to our souls that we have to harden our hearts against the promptings of the Spirit. Eventually, we harden our hearts against not only God, but all of His children. We lose the ability to feel selfless love, empathy, and compassion. Viewing pornography is spiritually damaging and is a sin. The act of lusting after another individual is inappropriate. When actively sought after, repentance and forgiveness require confession of all pornography use to an authorized servant of the Lord. Pornography decreases our sensitivity to the Spirit. It inhibits our judgment, and the desire for the next "fix" can cause individuals to make poor decisions which they would not

otherwise make. It has a tendency to cause users to try to minimize, lie about, or keep their actions secret—thus undermining their integrity. President Hinckley has stated:

Pornography, with its sleazy filth, sweeps over the earth like a horrible, engulfing tide. It is poison. Do not watch it or read it. It will destroy you if you do. It will take from you your self-respect. It will rob you of a sense of the beauties of life. It will tear you down and pull you into a slough of evil thoughts and possibly evil actions. Stay away from it. Shun it as you would a foul disease, for it is just as deadly.

—*Ensign*, NOV. 1997, p 51

Pornography Addiction Destroys Relationships

The following statistics have been reported regarding pornography: 56% of divorces involve pornography use;[18] pornography causes a 300% increase in the likelihood of infidelity;[19] 58% of addicts will suffer considerable financial loses;[20] and 33% of addicts lose their job because of pornography use.[21]

Learning About Healthy Sexuality And Our Bodies

It is important to learn about the true nature of the gifts from our Heavenly Father: our bodies and our sexuality. But pornography is not the way to do it. Pornography creates unhealthy expectations regarding sexuality. It is important to ask parents any questions

---

18: http://pornharms.com/full_article.php?article_no=384

19: Tom W. Smith; *American Sexual Behavior: Trends, Socio-Demographic Differences, and Risk Behavior; National Opinion Research Center; University of Chicago; GSS Topical Report No. 25; Updated December, 1998*

20: Judy Roberts, *"Porn: The Marriage Killer." Legatus Magazine; http://www.legatusmagazine.org/?p=2307&cpage=1*

21: Jennifer P. Schneider, MD, PhD; *How to Recognize the Signs of Sexual Addiction ;VOL 90/N0 6/NOVEMBER 1, 1991/POSTGRADUATE MEDICINE - SEXUAL ADDICTION; http://www.jenniferschneider.com/index.html*

Section

7

that you may have and learn about sexuality in the proper context of God's plan.

Suggested Activity

Discuss the handout "Comparing Healthy and Toxic Relationships" by Jill C. Manning, PhD in the Resources section of this manual.

Overcoming

If you are worried that you might be addicted to pornography and cannot seem to stop, are voluntarily viewing pornography, or have ping ponged back and forth between viewing and abstaining, it is very likely that you are addicted to pornography. First, come out of hiding and discuss your pornography addiction with your bishop and parents. This addiction needs secrecy and shame to survive; that's why the first step in addiction recovery is to bring the problem out into the open. Recovering from pornography addiction requires a full commitment to do whatever it takes to recover, but is possible. You must be completely and totally honest. Do not minimize the situation. Pornography addiction is a very serious problem.

Support

In the process of recovery, help and support are available. To gain real recovery—rather than just white knuckle abstinence—you need the support of a number of people. If you are struggling with pornography or are worried a friend might have a problem, talk with your bishop, be totally honest, and make arrangements to

meet weekly or even twice a week to honestly report on your progress. Your Church leaders will support you. Stay connected to them. Don't hide. Talk with your parents. They are part of your support team and can help you find the help and support you need to recover. Be honest if you are worried about yourself or another. However, do not share with everyone. Seek support selectively from people you completely trust (parents, Church leaders, counselors, and some friends).

Regular meetings with a qualified counselor, if at all possible, can help you discover your vulnerabilities and strengths and help you develop the emotional tools you need to combat this addiction. Most people who have fought this addiction say that their participation in a 12-Step addiction recovery group was essential for their recovery.

In addition to speaking with leaders and getting help, it is important to recognize the power of the Atonement. Accept the Atonement of Jesus Christ in your life. His Atonement is more powerful than our weaknesses. Focus your thoughts on Christ with more intensity than ever before. Consider the turning point for Alma the younger:[22]

> *16 And now, for three days and for three nights was I racked, even with the pains of a damned soul.*
>
> *17 And it came to pass that as I was thus racked with torment, while I was harrowed up by the memory of my many sins, behold, I remembered also to have heard my father prophesy unto the people concerning the coming of one Jesus Christ, a Son of God, to atone for the sins of the world.*
>
> *18 Now, as my mind caught hold upon this thought, I cried within my heart: O Jesus, thou Son of God, have mercy on me, who am in the gall of bitterness, and am encircled about by the*

22: Alma 36: 16-21

gall of bitterness, and am encircled about by the everlasting chains of death.

19 And now, behold, when I thought this, I could remember my pains no more; yea, I was harrowed up by the memory of my sins no more.

20 And oh, what joy, and what marvelous light I did behold; yea, my soul was filled with joy as exceeding as was my pain!

21 Yea, I say unto you, my son, that there could be nothing so exquisite and so bitter as were my pains. Yea, and again I say unto you, my son, that on the other hand, there can be nothing so exquisite and sweet as was my joy.

—ALMA 36:16-21

Conclusion

Long ago, prophets testified "that in the last days perilous times shall come."[23] Pornography is a perilous activity in our day. It has the power to destroy our lives, relationships, and the things we hold most dear, and devour our very spirits. However, the Lord has also said that "if ye are prepared ye shall not fear."[24] As we prepare ourselves spiritually and physically by turning to Christ, our leaders and parents, we do not need to fear. No matter our situation, they can help us find ways to avoid pornography and recover from any impact it has had on us.

23: *2 Timothy 3:1*
24: *D&C 38:30*

Section

7

Sample Lesson D: Developing Christlike Relationships That Lead to Marriage

Addressing the Problem of Pornography with Older Teenagers and Young Single Adults

- **Audience:** Teenagers and Young Single Adults, ages 16–30

- **Purpose:** To help young single adults understand the nature of pornography addiction, the recovery process, and how to develop healthy relationships free of pornography addiction

- **Outline:** (1) Introduction, (2) Prevention, (3) Dating, (4) Overcoming, and (5) Conclusion

Suggested Preparation

Carefully read the lesson and pray about what you should present. Review "Discussion Points for Young Single Adults" in the Discussing Pornography section. Read the relevant Personal Stories from the Resource section. Gather paper and pens for all those in the class. Prepare the chalkboard. Read through the Handouts in the Resources section and print off relevant handouts and Elder Holland's talk from the April, 2010 General Conference.[25]

25: Elder Jeffrey R. Holland, "Place No More for the Enemy of My Soul." April 2010 General Conference

Introduction

Suggested Activity

Have your young adults take a few moments to list the following: (1) what they most want in this life, (2) what they want in the life to come, and (3) what they are willing to sacrifice to obtain these objectives. Explain that Heavenly Father wants us to obtain the things that will bring us true happiness, but acquiring blessings requires effort on our part.

As children of God, we are on earth so that we might have joy. Three great gifts our Father in Heaven has given us are our bodies, our ability to procreate, and our agency. Some of the tools we have been given to help us obtain true happiness are physical bodies, families, and the ability to have a mortal experience so that we can become more like God. Elder Jeffrey R. Holland has told us that "...of all the titles God has chosen for Himself, *Father* is the one He favors most, and *creation* is His watchword. ...It is by becoming a father or mother that we are able to become like God. ...Sexual intimacy is...a union between mortals and deity."[26]

What we choose to do with our body affects our spirit and has eternal consequences. If we choose to, we can form eternal families that bring us joy and happiness. Something that has the ability to quickly destroy that union and inhibit our ability to obtain a fullness of joy and reach our eternal objectives is pornography. We must be bold about this topic. As we talk about pornography, think about how it affects what you most want in this life and what you want in the life to come.

Prevention

All of us need to be on guard about pornography. "The compromise available at the click of a mouse—including what can happen in a chat room's virtual encounter—is no respecter of persons, male or female, young or old, married or single."[27] Some statistics indicate that 87% of men ages 18–26 reported using pornography at some level.[28] While statistics for the LDS population are unknown, pornography is a problem for many active members of the Church. We all must carefully evaluate the influence of inappropriate material in our life. Some of the most powerful forms of prevention are to become educated, set high standards, and create habits that will lessen the impact of pornography.

26: Elder Jeffrey R. Holland, "Of Souls, Symbols, and Sacraments." BYU Devotional, Jan. 18, 1988

27: Elder Jeffrey R. Holland, "Place No More for the Enemy of My Soul." April 2010 General Conference

28: Jason Carroll and others, Generation XXX: Pornography Acceptance and Use Among Emerging Adults.

Pornography Education 101

Suggested Activity

Write the following questions and participants' answers on the board or paper.

Q: What is pornography?

A: Pornography is "material that is sexually explicit and intended primarily for the purpose of sexual arousal." It may depict nudity or sexual behavior. It may include materials such as romance novels, photographs, movies, electronic images, video games, Internet chat rooms, erotic telephone conversations, music, or other media.

Q: Is pornography addictive?

A: Pornography is like alcohol or drugs in that it can be extremely addictive. Viewing pornography can actually cause a depletion of dopamine in our brains, which causes simple pleasures to no longer be enough, and causes the addict to continually seek pornography and act out in addiction.[29] Pornography often leads to inappropriate sexual behavior with oneself or with others. Elder Dallin H. Oaks has warned us that "pornography is... addictive. It impairs decision-making capacities and it 'hooks' its users, drawing them back obsessively for more and more."[30]

Q: Why should I care about pornography?

A: Pornography absolutely mocks and scorns the precious gifts our Father in Heaven has given us: our bodies and our ability to procreate. Its use also causes addiction, which robs us of our free will. Viewing pornography is so painful to our souls that we have to harden our hearts against the promptings of the Spirit. Eventually, we harden our hearts against not only God, but all His children. We lose the ability to feel selfless love, empathy, and compassion. We may lose all that is godly within us.

29: Donald L. Hilton, Jr., MD, He Restoreth My Soul, p 72.

30: Elder Dallin H. Oaks, "Pornography," Ensign May 2005

Viewing pornography is spiritually damaging and is a sin.[31] It decreases our sensitivity to the Spirit. It inhibits our judgment, and the desire for the next "fix" can cause individuals to make poor decisions they would not otherwise make.[32] Pornography users tend to try to minimize, lie about, or keep their actions secret, thus undermining their integrity. It has been the cause of jeopardizing many individuals' jobs and financial security. It is a substantial reason for many divorces. Viewing pornography often escalates to other inappropriate behaviors.

Q: How does pornography affect relationships?

A: Pornography damages our ability to have happy, fulfilling relationships with others. Elder Richard G. Scott said pornography "…is one of the most damning influences on earth."[33] When we are "damned," our progression is stopped.[34] In this life, one of the most important steps we can take to progress eternally is to be sealed in the temple. Addiction to pornography stops our progression by preventing us from worthily entering the temple. It also represents the antithesis of the kind of actions required to preserve and grow an eternal relationship. When we use pornography we are not thinking of Jesus Christ or others, but of our own immediate selfish gratification. "If we stop chopping at the branches of this problem and strike more directly at the root of the tree, not surprisingly we find lust lurking furtively there."[35]

Lust is deadly because it not only is completely spirit-destroying, but it "defiles the highest and holiest relationship God gives us in mortality."[36] Pornography objectifies people and inhibits our ability to be sensitive to and connect with them. We begin to see other people as objects instead of children of God. Pornography use encourages unhealthy and distorted views about sexuality. Pornography is a powerful tool used by the adversary to keep us from marrying, from having happy families, and from living fulfilling lives. It can literally stop our eternal progression and ability to participate in God's plan.

Suggested Activity

Discuss the Comparing Healthy and Toxic Relationships chart in the Handout section of this manual. Also, discuss Elder Jeffrey R. Holland's talk *"Place No More for the Enemy of My Soul,"*[37] and the comparisons he makes between *lust* and *love*.

- ◈ Setting High Standards and Creating Good Habits: The prevalence of pornographic material in media makes it expedient for all individuals to take active measures to protect themselves.[38] Choose movies and media carefully. Set standards and be accountable to others.

- ◈ Practice Internet safety by installing filters and placing computers in safe places.

- ◈ Consider the type of clothing you wear and the material you pass around or joke about.

- ◈ If you accidentally see pornography, discuss it with a leader, parent, or friend immediately.

31: *Elder Holland, "Place No More for the Enemy of My Soul," April 2010 General Conference.*

32: *Donald L. Hilton, Jr., MD, He Restoreth My Soul, p 71.*

33: *Elder Scott, "To Acquire Spiritual Guidance," October 2009 General Conference.*

34: *Damnation is the opposite of salvation, and exists in varying degrees. All who do not obtain the fulness of celestial exaltation will to some degree be limited in their progress and privileges, and hence be damned to that extent." Bible Dictionary, Damnation.*

35: *Elder Holland, "Place No More for the Enemy of My Soul," April 2010 General Conference.*

36: *Ibid*

37: *Elder Holland, "Place No More for the Enemy of My Soul," April 2010 General Conference.*

38: *Elder Holland has said, "start by separating yourself from people, materials, and circumstances that will harm you." Unwelcome thoughts can come, but "we don't have to throw open the door, serve them tea and crumpets, and then tell them where the silverware is kept!"*

⬧ Think of how viewing pornography will hurt those you love. Elder Holland said, "Surely it would guide our actions in a dramatic way if we remembered that every time we transgress, we hurt not only those we love, but we also hurt Him, who so dearly loves us."

Dating and Pornography

Being casual about and failing to address the issue of pornography when seriously dating someone can have serious spiritual and physical implications for you and your future family. Pornography is a common problem that can have a negative impact on a marriage and family life. It is not wise to assume the person whom you are dating has not been exposed to pornography; we all have. There are sweet sisters and wonderful returned missionaries who are addicted to pornography. The problem does not go away after marriage. It may temporarily halt, but then resurface and become an even more serious problem if left untreated. By openly discussing pornography use, much can be done to safeguard yourself and your relationship. This can allow you to better know how to proceed with the relationship and to establish patterns and behaviors to protect you and your future family. Even if you are not currently dating someone, it is important to start thinking about how you might approach this topic now.

When should I discuss pornography with the person I am dating? The following are some factors you may consider in determining when to discuss this topic: Are you dating? Is the relationship such that you can talk about, or have already talked about other significant personal issues? Are you looking to advance your relationship by getting engaged or married? If you can answer "yes" to one or more of those questions, it may be an appropriate time to discuss pornography. Discuss the topic before getting engaged or married.

How should I discuss pornography? This is a topic that needs to be addressed more than once. For many, discussing pornography is uncomfortable. Be sensitive and respectful while asking, listening to, and responding to the other person. If your boyfriend is

viewing pornography, he may have never told anyone. Unless he feels love, your boyfriend may not share personal information. Be sensitive to the Spirit when discerning whether your boyfriend is telling the truth or minimizing behavior. If your boyfriend is using pornography, there is a good chance he will downplay his behavior. If your boyfriend has a problem, lovingly suggest that he get help. These are some questions you might ask: How have you been exposed to pornography? Have you actively sought pornography before? What were the circumstances and the frequency of use? When did you last seek pornography? Do you consider your pornography use as a problem? What actions have you taken to stop or protect yourself from pornography in the past?

Suggested Activity

Role play how you might discuss pornography in a simple, straightforward manner with the person you are dating.

Q: What factors should I consider when deciding whether to continue a relationship with someone who has been or is addicted to pornography?

A: Do not underestimate the damaging effects of pornography use. Carefully consider the implications of dating those who are not actively seeking recovery. Research has shown that it can take 7–12 months before an addict can begin to obtain solid sobriety, and even then, it can take 2–5 years to gain solid recovery and heal from an addiction's effects. Just because someone is not currently viewing pornography does not mean that a past problem will not resurface in the future. However, recovery is possible, and those who actively seek help can find healing.

Some questions you may consider in making dating decisions might include: Is your partner open and honest about his pornography usage? What steps were and are being taken to recover from pornography? How long has he gone without viewing pornography? Has your partner healed from the effects of pornography addiction? Ultimately, it is important to rely on the Spirit when making these decisions.

Section

7

Recognizing and Overcoming Pornography

Q: How can I tell if I have a problem with pornography?

A: If you keep telling yourself not to look at pornography and find yourself doing so anyway, you have a problem. Don't minimize the situation. You need to be completely honest and get help. Have you been totally honest with your bishop when you have voluntarily viewed pornography? If you have seen pornography and it has bothered you, or you think you have a problem, talk with your parents. Your parents love you and can help you find the help you need. Actions done in secrecy and shame need to be honestly addressed.

Q: Is recovery possible?

A: If you are struggling with pornography or lust, know that the Atonement is real. Faith in Jesus Christ means confidence in His power to heal us.[39] The physical chains of pornography addiction are strong and you will need help to break them. Facing addiction and admitting or disclosing behavior is the first and most important step. Talk with your parents and your bishop. Become educated regarding addiction and the recovery process, set boundaries, find a good therapist, and attend a 12-Step support addiction recovery group. 12-Step programs have been reported by many to be one of the most important elements in the recovery process. A good 12-Step addiction recovery group provides a sponsor, a support group, and a program to work on a daily basis. All of these are essential to solid recovery.

Q: As a recovering addict, what factors should I consider while dating seriously?

A: Graphic details are not necessary, but tell the person you are dating the nature and extent of your exposure to pornography and related behaviors. It is often recommended that you should be well along in the recovery process before entering into a serious relationship. If you are receiving counseling or attending 12-Step groups, the person you are dating may consider also meeting with the counselor or attending a 12-Step support program.

Conclusion

Consider again what you most want and how pornography use and lust could affect your life. Now write what you will do to keep pornography out of your life and to form healthy relationships. As we follow the Spirit and take active measures, we can protect ourselves and heal from the prevalent influence of pornography in our society.

39: Elder Holland, *"Place No More for the Enemy of My Soul,"* April 2010 General Conference.

Sample Lesson E: Replacing Fear with Faith

Exercising Courage While Dealing with the Difficult Topic of Pornography

- **Audience:** General Audience

- **Purpose:** To help individuals, spouses, and parents learn to recognize ways they can effectively prevent and handle pornography addiction and resulting behaviors

- **Outline:** (1) Introduction, (2) Prevention, (3) Recognition, (4) Overcoming/Support, and (5) Conclusion

Suggested Preparation

Carefully read the lesson and pray about what you should present. Read "Discussion Points for Adults" in the Discussing Pornography section. Read the relevant "Personal Stories" in the Resources section and review the Handouts in the Resources section of this manual.

Introduction

Pornography is extremely prevalent in the world around us and can have devastating effects. However, we do not need to fear.[40] As we prepare ourselves by becoming educated, exercising faith, and relying

on the Spirit, we will be equipped to appropriately address the problem of pornography. We are on the Lord's side, and His side will prevail. His forces are mightier than those of the adversary.

Prevention

Some of the most important things that can be done to guard against pornography addiction are to become educated, exercise faith, set high personal standards, and take active measures as guided by the Spirit to protect against this problem in your home.

40: D&C 38:30

Section

7

1. Become educated. It is important to become aware of the problem.

Know the extent of the problem. Exposure to pornography starts much earlier than many think. Some statistics indicate that the average age of exposure is 11 years old[41] and that almost all males will be exposed by the time they are 14 years old.[42] 47% of families in the United States say pornography is a problem in their home.[43] Although exact numbers for those in the Church are unknown, many LDS people struggle with pornography addiction.

Elder Dallin H. Oaks shares this experience: "Pornography is also addictive. It impairs decision-making capacities and it 'hooks' its users, drawing them back obsessively for more and more. A man who had been addicted to pornography and to hard drugs wrote me this comparison: 'In my eyes cocaine doesn't hold a candle to this. I have done both. …Quitting even the hardest drugs was nothing compared to [trying to quit pornography].'" One definition of addiction is "the use of a substance or activity for the purpose of lessening pain or augmenting pleasure by a person who has lost control over the rate, frequency or duration of its use and whose life has become progressively unmanageable as a result." Some indicators that an individual has become addicted include the desire for increased stimulus (harder or more frequent exposure), frequent relapses, and the inability to stop behavior despite negative consequences. When individuals become addicted to pornography, physical changes occur in the brain. Chemicals released in the brain create dependency on the continued viewing of pornography. The prefrontal cortex shrinks, impairing moral judgment and reasoning.

The addictive nature of pornography almost always leads to other acting out behaviors on some level. These may include masturbation, lying, inappropriate sexual activity, prostitution, abuse, domestic violence, and other crimes.

Viewing pornography is spiritually damaging. It inhibits our judgment, and the desire for the next "fix" can cause individuals to make poor decisions they would not otherwise make.[44] Those addicted to pornography often try to minimize the seriousness of or hide their actions, thus undermining their integrity.

Pornography damages lives and relationships. Some statistics indicate that 40% of men viewing pornography lose their spouses,[45] 50% of those viewing pornography will suffer significant financial losses,[46] and 33% of pornography users will lose their jobs.[47] Pornography use also increases the chance of infidelity by 300%.[48]

2. Exercise faith. Replace fear with faith and call upon the powers of Heaven for assistance.

With honesty and humility, call upon the powers of heaven for discernment and assistance. Replace fear with faith. In April General Conference, 2010, Julie B. Beck said, "The ability to qualify for, receive, and act on personal revelation is the single most important skill that can be acquired in this life. Qualifying for the Lord's Spirit begins with a desire for that Spirit and implies a certain degree of worthiness." Have confidence in your personal ability to know what to do. If you let the Spirit be your guide and teacher, you will know what to do.

3. Set high personal standards.

Carefully evaluate personal appearances and media. Act with virtue and exhibit modesty. Everyone can help prevent pornography by acting with virtue and exhibiting modesty. Elder M. Russell Ballard said that women "…need to understand that when they wear clothing that is too tight, too short, or too low cut, they not only can send the wrong message to young men

41: Jerry Roplato, Internet Pornography Statistics, http://internet-filter-review.toptenreviews.com/internet-pornography-statistics.html

42: Jill C. Manning. What's the Big Deal About Pornography?, Shadow Mountain, SLC, UT 2008

43: http://purefamily.org/child-pornography-statistics.html

44: Donald L. Hilton, Jr., MD, He Restoreth My Soul, pg. 71.

45: Fagan, 2009, "Affects of Pornography on Individuals, Marriage, Family and Community," Research Synthesis Journal

46: http://www.articlesbase.com/addictions-articles/reasons-for-internet-pornography-addiction-875433.html

47: Jennifer P. Schneider, MD, PhD; How to recognize the signs of sexual addiction ;VOL 90/N0 6/NOVEMBER 1, 1991/POSTGRADUATE MEDICINE - SEXUAL ADDICTION; http://www.jenniferschneider.com/index.html

48: http://lifegems4marriage.com/2010/04/02/porn-use-increases-infidelity-divorce/

with whom they associate, but they also perpetuate in their own minds the fallacy that a woman's value is dependent solely on her sensual appeal. This never has been nor will it ever be within the righteous definition of a faithful daughter of God."[49] It is imperative that individuals exhibit modesty and teach those in their sphere of influence to do the same.

Consider media viewed. Elder David A. Bednar has pleaded with us to "...be careful of becoming so immersed and engrossed in pixels, texting, earbuds, twittering, online social networking, and potentially addictive uses of media and the Internet that [we] fail to recognize the importance of [our] physical bod[ies] and miss the richness of person-to-person communication."[50] Evaluate time used in virtual settings, particularly with friends of the opposite sex in chat rooms, online gaming, Facebook, role-playing games, etc. Individuals should carefully consider the frequency of media use as well as the media's content. Many television shows, movies, and games contain sexual and pornographic content.

4. Take active measures to protect your home

Become educated, install filters on computers, be aware of the problem, teach your children about healthy sexuality, and ask them to tell you if they see inappropriate material.

49: Julie B. Beck, "Mothers and Daughters," Ensign, May 2010
50: David A. Bednar, "Things As They Really Are," Ensign, June 2010

Recognition

How can I tell if a loved one has a pornography problem? There are some indicators which may be helpful in identifying if someone has a problem with pornography.[51] Some behaviors that may be associated with viewing pornography are lying, selfishness, denial, isolation, avoidance, hiding, secretiveness, becoming emotionally checked out, procrastinating, and objectifying others. The best way to identify if there is a problem is to discuss concerns with the individual.

Q: How do I discuss pornography?

A: Use a direct approach, such as saying "I have noticed that . . ." and then name specific behaviors that are causing concern. If the individual denies any involvement or is defensive, respond with a peaceful, determined attitude. If the individual does disclose a problem, listen with compassion and concern. Therapist Michael D. Gardner, LDSFS, has stated:

> *Calmly and with love and support, encourage your spouse [or other individual] to fully disclose the extent of their addictive behavior rather than allowing information to trickle in over time. It is important for the type of addictive behavior, its duration, and its frequency to be disclosed. Take care not to jump to conclusions, "catastrophize," over-generalize, or get stuck in all-or-nothing thinking.*
>
> —"Hope, Healing and Dealing With Addiction," Ensign, May 2010

Q: How can I tell if I am addicted to pornography?

A: Simply put, if you keep telling yourself that you will stop viewing pornography, and you do not, then you are addicted to pornography. Addicts frequently experience a cycle of preoccupation with pornography followed by

---

51: See www.salifeline.org.

Section 7

ritualizing, acting out, and shame, which leads to repeating the cycle.

Q: How can I tell if I need help as the spouse or parent of an addict?

A: The addictive behavior of individuals impacts those around them. Spouses of addicts frequently experience symptoms similar to post-traumatic stress disorder which includes sleeplessness, confusion, indecisiveness, loss of appetite or overeating, fatigue, depression, and uncontrolled emotion. Additionally, loved ones of addicts frequently experience shock, denial, and anger, which all can lead to a cycle of feeling fear, obsessing over another's addiction, and experiencing shame. If, as the loved one of an addict, you are experiencing any of these symptoms or otherwise feel that your life is unmanageable, you may consider seeking help.

Overcome and Support

If you are struggling with pornography addiction, there is hope. The scriptures teach that as individuals humble themselves and look to Christ, the Atonement will work in their lives.[52] However, recovery almost always requires that the addicted individual get help. Elder Holland said that "…people bound by the chains of true addictions often need more help than self-help."[53]

Q: What are the elements of recovery?

A: Individuals must desire recovery. Recovery requires: (1) honestly disclosing behavior to your ecclesiastical leader and spouse, (2) becoming educated about sexual addiction, (3) setting boundaries, (4) using therapy/counseling, and (5) following the 12-Step program. "Start by separating yourself from people, materials, and circumstances that will harm you"[54] and by being honest with others. Do not wait to speak with

your spouse, parents, or bishop. Set rules regarding computer or television use, and set other boundaries. Go to a 12-Step meeting now.

Q: What is recovery?

A: True recovery requires more than just ceasing to view pornography. It requires having a change of heart. It is a lifestyle change wherein the individual fully commits to all steps of recovery. Some visible changes of recovery are that humility replaces pride, gratitude replaces resentment and anger, self-respect replaces guilt, and a desire to help others in similar circumstances replaces a desire to hide past behavior.

Q: What about loved ones surrounding the addict?

A: Many fail to realize the need for spouses, parents, and others closely surrounding the addict to get help and heal. If you are the spouse or a loved one of an addict, recognize your own need for healing. Speak with your bishop and trusted individuals about your situation. Make sure that you get support. Dr. Jill C. Manning teaches the CAVED theory. Those who are afflicted need Connection, Advocacy, Validation, Education, and Direction.[55]

Recognize that the addiction of a loved one is not your fault or responsibility. You cannot fix or control

52: Alma 34:31

53: Elder Jeffrey R. Holland, "Place No More for the Enemy of My Soul," Ensign, May 2010

54: Ibid.

55: Jill C. Manning, Wendy L. Watson (2008) Sexual Addiction and Compulsivity, vol. 15, p. 233-249

him.[56] "Establishing boundaries differs from issuing ultimatums in an attempt to control the other person's behavior. Recovering spouses determine which behaviors are unacceptable to them and what they will do if those behaviors occur. Knowing the consequences, the addict can then choose what he wishes to do. Realistic boundaries cannot be established until ones' self esteem is high enough to place ones' own needs above the need to please the spouse." However, you can set boundaries to protect yourself and the relationship. "People without boundaries respond automatically to the anger of others. They rescue, seek approval, or get angry themselves…. Do not let an out of control person be the cue for you to change your course."[57] Recognize and break co-dependency cycles. Support recovery action, but refuse to enable addictive behavior such as lying, anger, defensiveness, playing victim, and remaining emotionally distant.

Slow down and take care of yourself by getting adequate rest, exercise, nutrition, and support. Become educated regarding pornography addiction and the recovery process. Find a qualified therapist. Attend 12-Step support group meetings regularly, get a sponsor, and work the steps of recovery on a daily basis.

Q: How can we heal our relationship?

56: *Jennifer Schneider, Dr. Rebuilding the Marriage during Recovery from Compulsive Sexual Behavior,* Family Relations Journal.

57: *Dr. Henry Cloud, John Townsend,* Boundaries. *(1992) Zondervan, Grand Rapids, Michigan*

A: Recovery of the relationship is based on both individuals doing the work of their own recovery. Allow time (usually one year minimum unless you are in danger) for your spouse to make lifestyle changes and decide if they will demonstrate full commitment to the necessary recovery actions. This is different than just abstaining from addict behavior. Healing is a spiritual process. Believe that Jesus Christ can restore you and your loved one to wholeness. Turn your life over to your Heavenly Father and Jesus Christ.

Conclusion

Recovery for both addicts and their spouses is a spiritual process. The power that comes from accepting the Atonement in one's life is the only way to find peace, healing, and wholeness. We live in a time when many resources are available to help us effectively handle this epidemic. As individuals become educated and take appropriate action to protect and heal their families as guided by the Spirit, they will be inspired regarding how to best help themselves and those who are struggling and how to protect their families and homes.

Handouts

Handouts available from SA Lifeline at *www.salifeline.org/bookstore* can be used with lessons or independently. Samples, which can be copied for non-commercial use, are included here in this section:

- ❖ *Recovery and Healing from the Effects of Pornography and Sexual Addiction* (available as a Pamphlet)

- ❖ *Dating and Pornography* (available as a Pamphlet)

- ❖ *The Family Fight Against Pornography* (available as a Pamphlet)

- ❖ *Young Single Adult Pledge*

- ❖ *Family Pledge*

- ❖ *Contrasting Healthy Sexuality and Pornographic Portrayals of Sexuality* (Chart)

- ❖ *Comparing Healthy and Toxic Relationships* (Chart)

- ❖ *Am I Serious About Dealing with My Pornography Problem?* (Chart)

- ❖ *Am I Making Effective Changes to Deal with My Spouse's Pornography Problem?* (Chart)

- ❖ *Common Terms*

Section

8

Recovery and Healing from the effects of Pornography & Sexual Addiction

For the Individual • For the Spouse • For the Marriage

If life is compared to a river, it is easy to imagine floating with the current gently down the stream. But, if we simply go with the flow, disaster awaits. Every worthy goal takes constant, if gentle, effort to move upstream and each individual must take responsibility for rowing their own boat if success is to be obtained.

So it is with sexual addiction and marriage—each person must take responsibility for their own recovery. Recognize that individual effort and commitment is required, both for the addict and the afflicted spouse. While each can support the personal recovery of the other, ultimately each person is responsible for their own success. Only then is there hope that the relationship can recover and the marriage can move gently up the stream.

"Our message is one of hope. Honestly seek recovery and you will find it."
—Steven & Rhyll Croshaw
Founders of
SA Lifeline Foundation

GENTLY UP THE STREAM *by* Linda Curley Christensen
(used with permission)

Recovery for an *Individual*

Goal: *Restore self-respect, connection with God, and wholeness*

Decide to Fully Commit to Actions of Recovery

- Recognize the reality of pornography/sexual addiction.
- Progress will occur when a decision is made to fully commit to actions of recovery.
- Seek Gods help, He will help you.

Come Out of Hiding

- Complete, honest disclosure to spouse, clergy leader, and qualified therapist is necessary.

Set Safe Boundaries and Self Care

- Set safe boundaries (for example, no private computer or television use).
- Daily physical and spiritual care: exercise, healthy diet, adequate rest, positive affirmations.

Gain Knowledge

- Learn about sexual addiction.
- Learn what recovery requires and the attributes of genuine recovery.
- Short-term sobriety (abstinence) does not indicate recovery. Full recovery is a life-time process.
- Learn how to support your spouse's healing.

Clergy Involvement

- Frequent accountability visits with an informed ecclesiastical leader.

Qualified Counseling

- Genuine commitment to on-going counseling from a qualified therapist. (Typical minimum is 18 months).

Join 12- Step Fellowship for Sexual Addiction Recovery

- Join a 12-Step Fellowship for sexual addiction, find a sponsor, work all 12 steps. Commit to long-term, perhaps lifetime involvement.

Recovery is a Spiritual Process

- Willingly acknowledge that alone a person is powerless over their addiction.
- Come to believe that a Power greater than oneself can restore wholeness to life.
- We must turn our will and life over to that Power.

Saving the *Marriage*

Goal: *Restore connection and wholeness*

Recognize the Marriage Relationship Is Affected

- Trust has been violated. The marriage may be intact, but it is not whole. If the marriage relationship is recoverable, it will not happen immediately.
- Genuine recovery of a marriage relationship takes time. There is no universal rule regarding how long it will take. Follow your instincts.
- If you desire to save your marriage, seek out a qualified counselor trained in sexual addiction.

Working on Recovery Allows Marriage to Heal

- A healthy, whole marriage cannot co-exist with sexually addictive behavior. If the addiction continues, the marriage will never be whole—the addiction will always win.

Work on Individual Recovery and Healing

- Recovery of the marriage relationship follows continued individual recovery and healing from the trauma of addiction.

Reach Out to Each Other

- Notice ways in which your spouse is trying to reach out for connection. Respond to such efforts with honesty.

Build True Intimacy

- In recovery, a one-dimensional physical relationship is replaced with an intimate social, emotional, spiritual, and sexual bonding.
- Spend time together to develop a holistic relationship (walking, gardening, cooking, etc.).

Nurture Others

- Children need extra love and attention. They may also be suffering and are in need of healing.
- Needed personal renewal will be found in small acts of service.

Healing for the Afflicted *Spouse*

Goal: Restore serenity and wholeness

Recognize Your Own Need for Healing

- Recognize your trauma as an afflicted spouse of an individual addicted to pornography.
- Seek God's help, He will help you.

Talk with Others

- Interact with an ecclesiastical leader.
- Communicate with a qualified therapist.
- Develop a support system.

Join a 12-Step Fellowship

- Find a sponsor, work all 12 steps diligently.

Self Care

- Slow down. Allow time for healing before making life changing decisions (1 year minimum). If you are at risk, decisions may need to happen more quickly.
- Prayerfully set boundaries defining unacceptable behavior to protect your emotional, physical, and spiritual well-being.
- Daily physical and spiritual care: exercise, healthy diet, adequate rest, spiritually centering activities.

Education

- Fully recognize that you are not the cause of your spouse's addiction, and that you cannot "fix" or control your spouse.
- Learn more about the nature of pornography/sexual addiction and how it impacts you.
- Learn what is required to experience healing as the spouse of one addicted.

Support Spouse's Recovery

- Make very clear to your spouse that you will support his/her genuine commitment to recovery, but will not enable continued addictive behaviors.

Healing is a Spiritual Process

- Willingly acknowledge that you are powerless over your spouse's actions. You can influence, but you cannot control.
- Believe that a Power greater than you can restore you to wholeness. Turn your life over to that Power.

Pornography 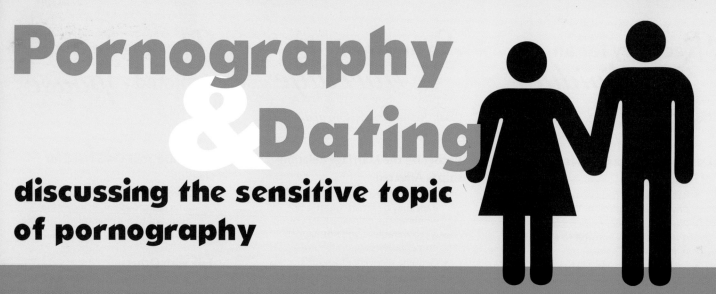 & Dating

discussing the sensitive topic of pornography

why should i talk about porn with those i date?

Everyone has been exposed to porn. Exposure can motivate a person to actively and repeatedly seek out porn to fulfill sexual desire. This constant consumption is addictive, causing a hormonal release that affects the brain in a way similar to cocaine. Besides creating a dependency, porn changes how we value our bodies, relationships, view others, and is a destructive force in dating and marriage.

Discussing porn with those we date allows us to ascertain another's history of porn exposure, consumption and their attitude towards actively seeking out porn. Opening up communication and establishing mutual expectations can help guide relationship decisions. Especially when developing a serious relationship, discussing porn can help establish rules to protect your relationship and future family.

what if the person i am dating views porn?

While you should appreciate their willingness to share delicate information, don't underestimate porn. Become educated and carefully weigh the emotional risks. Ending an addiction is a grueling process that takes significant commitment and time (usually 7–12 months abstinence to start gaining recovery), and often involves sporadic relapses. Changing attitudes and behaviors can take years. As you gauge how this problem affects your relationship, assess the person's willingness to stop. What recovery steps are being taken? What further ones will they take?

Consider setting rules regarding the progression or continuance of the relationship. Speak with other trusted individuals, such as family, counselors and close friends, to gain perspective. Supporting recovery is helpful; policing another's addictive behavior is not. Attend counseling together or a twelve–step support group if appropriate.

when should i have this discussion?

Porn is a sensitive topic. Nonetheless, it is important to discuss porn early on as you become emotionally committed in the relationship. Porn should be brought up on more than one occasion and on varioups levels depending on the commitment level of the relationship. Closeness and relationship expectations can guide these discussions.

what should i say?

Share the importance of open communication and the care you have for the other person. Then bring up the need to discuss pornography despite the awkwardness of the topic. Items should be discussed that honestly explore both of your histories in terms of porn exposure, consumption, and attitudes towards porn. If a problem arose in the past or continues in the present, mention what actions are or have been taken to fix it. Useful questions could be:

• How have you been exposed to porn?

• Have you actively sought porn?

• If so, what was the frequency and surrounding circumstances?

• When did you last seek porn?

• Do you view porn as a problem?

• What actions have you taken to stop or protect yourself from porn in the past? the future?

what if i currently have a porn addiction?

While it may seem best to hide this problem, get help and recognize that honest, open disclosure to trusted individuals is crucial in overcoming this addiction. It is critical to learn about the nature of porn addiction, and the areas in which it disrupts your life. Help yourself by assessing the circumstances surrounding porn usage and strive to remove them.

Overcoming pornography requires a strong commitment and desire to recover. Commit to on-going counseling from a qualified therapist (typically 18+ months). Join a 12-step fellowship for porn addiction where you can gain a sponsor who can help you through the recovery steps. You may wish to commit to long term involvement. Religious persons have found frequent visits with an ecclesiastical leader and communion with God to be essential to their recovery.

what about dating if i have a porn problem?

Recognize that honesty is crucial in serious dating. Keep in mind the length of the recovery process and the probability of relapse. Consider how these interface with your partner's expectations and the speed with which the relationship develops. Be upfront about your struggle and share the actions being taken to correct the issue.

The Family Fight Against Pornography

INFORMATION FOR PARENTS

"Internet pornography is a stealth attack on our homes and families through invisibly transmitted electrons. Education about the addictive, destructive nature of this attack is paramount".

Donald L. Hilton Jr., MD
Author of *He Restoreth My Soul*

Does My Family Need to be Concerned About Pornography?

LDS young men and women who are impacted by pornography addiction are often exceptional young people. They are student leaders, athletes, young men and women who are preparing for or returning from missions, and children of good parents. They may also be children with poor social skills or low self-esteem. There is a high probability that they are your children and your children's friends.

11 years old is the average age at which children first see online pornography.

Nearly 9 out of 10 (87%) young men, and 1 out of 3 (31%) young women report viewing pornography.

70% of men age 18–34 visit pornography websites in a typical month.

Parents cannot completely prevent their children's exposure to pornography. If this isn't something your kids are talking to you about, you need to start the discussion soon!

Prevention

- Make certain that computers are kept in high-traffic areas and have effective internet filters installed.

- Don't allow computer or cell phone use in bedrooms. At night, personal cell phones should be handed to parents for recharging.

- Have regular one-on-one discussions with your children. In these conversations teach your children about (age appropriate) healthy sexuality, the nature of God's gifts of our bodies, marriage-centered chastity, and the dangers of pornography. (The resources on the back of this brochure provide important information for parents on these topics).

- During your Family Home Evening, have a time where the kids can talk about some of "life's challenges" that they faced during the week. Encourage them to be open and express their feelings.

The Problem

Pornography is the most common addiction among LDS populations. Virtually all teens over the age of 16 have been exposed to pornography. Many who are exposed keep going back to it—even though they know it is wrong, feel ashamed, and are shocked by the images and videos they view.

For many children, teens, and young adults, education about sexuality comes from their peers, TV, movies, and from viewing pornography. This "education" is devoid of moral values and does not recognize sexuality as a God-given gift.

Realistically speaking, prevention measures alone are not enough to protect children from pornography. Parents need to teach their children that two of the greatest gifts the Lord has given them are their bodies and human sexuality.

Pornography is one of Satan's most effective tools. It degrades and mocks the divine creation of the human body and the gift of procreation. As with all of Satan's deceptions, pornography is a counterfeit of God's gifts and causes pain to the soul of man, destroys relationships, and distances one from God.

Recognizing and Combating Pornography Addiction

Signs of Pornography Addiction

- Repeatedly accessing pornography in spite of negative consequences
- Emotionally disconnected
- Anger, depression, critical, hostile, judgmental
- Withdrawing from family relationships, friends, church, activities

Combating Pornography Addiction

- Pornography addiction is a spiritual, emotional, and physical addiction
- Pornography addiction cannot be conquered through willpower and spiritual efforts alone
- Pornography addiction thrives in secrecy and shame—and will escalate over time
- Successful recovery requires working with a qualified counselor, frequent meetings with a bishop, education, and, for those 18 and older, attending a LDS PASG group and/or a 12 Step Sexaholics Anonymous group.
- Understand that *recovery* isn't "white knuckle" abstinence. Recovery from pornography addiction requires a change of heart and a lifestyle change.

Essential Reading & Resources

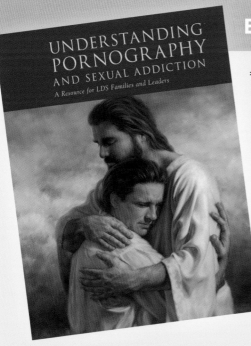

Understanding Pornography and Sexual Addiction: A Resource for LDS Families and Leaders. Produced and distributed by the SA Lifeline Foundation

He Restoreth My Soul: Understanding and Breaking the Chemical and Spiritual Chains of Pornography Addiction Through the Atonement of Jesus Christ. —Donald L. Hilton, Jr., MD

A Parent's Guide —www.lds.org

What's the Big Deal About Pornography? A Guide for the Internet Generation. —Jill C. Manning, Ph.D.

How to Talk to Your Child About Sex. —Linda and Richard Eyre

Growing Up: Gospel Answers About Maturation and Sex. —Brad Wilcox

Safeguarding Teens and Young adults from Pornography —Jason Carroll Ph.D. DVD; Produced by SA Lifeline Foundation

Available online at www.salifeline.org | Email: info@salifeline.org

This pamphlet is produced and published by the SA Lifeline Foundation, a non-profit 501(c)3 organization dedicated to fighting pornography through pornography addiction education and support for recovery. The Foundation is neither sponsored nor endorsed by The Church of Jesus Christ of Latter-day Saints.

My *Pledge*
to Fight the Plague

I commit that I will not be part of the pornographic plague. I will do this by:

- Educating myself on the harmful effects of pornography to self, spouse, and future family.

- Learning to recognize the red flags associated with pornography use, so that I can enter into relationships that are pornography free.

- Engaging in an open, honest conversation about pornography with those I choose to seriously date.

- Choosing to date only those who are willing to get help and purge their lives of pornographic materials.

- Seeking help from my ecclesiastical leaders if I am involved in pornography use.

- Refraining from engagement or marriage until a pornography problem is resolved. I recognize resolving the problem must be accompanied by a change of attitude and behavior, including seven to twelve months of sobriety.

I recognize these choices will lead to healthier and happier relationships with my future family.

_____
Signature   Date

Our Clean & Safe Media

Pledge

As a family, we commit to making safe media choices in order to protect our family and keep our home a happy and healthy place to be.

We will do this by:

- Selecting books, websites, music, magazines, activities and/or movies which are in harmony with our family values.
- Being kind to ourselves and to others by not posting or forwarding anything that could cause hurt, embarrassment or offense. If we receive a text or email that makes us feel uncomfortable, sad or scared, we will tell a parent right away.
- Showing respect for our body and others' bodies by not looking at or posting nude or immodest images. If we accidentally come across something inappropriate, we will tell a parent immediately.
- Protecting identifying information by not posting phone numbers, addresses or personal information in places where they could be seen by strangers. If we are unsure, we will ask a parent before posting personal information.
- Never meeting up with someone we have met online unless a parent knows exactly where we are and someone accompanies us.
- Limiting our media use when it is late at night or we are home alone.

_____   _____

_____   _____

_____   _____

_____   _____

Dated: _____

Contrasting Healthy Sexuality and Pornographic Portrayals of Sexuality

Prepared by Jill Manning, Ph.D.

Many people erroneously think of pornography as a substitute or preparation for healthy sexual relations. Healthy sexuality and intimacy, however, stand in sharp contrast to pornographic portrayals of sexuality. If left unchecked, pornography use can even hinder a person's ability to develop an intimate relationship and experience satisfying sexual relations in marriage. The following table is intended to help clarify some of the main differences between pornographic portrayals of sexuality and healthy sexuality.

Pornographic Portrayals of Sexuality	Healthy Sexuality
Lustful	Loving
Public	Private
Isolating	Unifying
Deceptive	Honest
Fantasy-based	Anchored in reality
Body is treated as an object, toy, or weapon	Body is sacred
Decreases well-being	Enhances well-being
Degrading	Respectful and honorable
Involves using or harming someone	Involves loving someone
Spiritually deadening	Spiritually meaningful
Socially irresponsible and costly	Socially responsible and beneficial
Often involves violence and coercion	Involves mutual consent and volition
Associated with crime, abuse, infidelity, addiction, prostitution, and divorce	Associated with life and joy

Comparing Healthy & Toxic Relationships

Prepared by Jill Manning, Ph.D.

When seeking a partner to date or marry, it is helpful to understand the differences between healthy and toxic relationships. All relationships experience ups and downs, but ideally, the majority of interactions with your partner will be in the healthy realm. When you consider the qualities listed in each column below, evaluate which side of the spectrum the majority of interactions with your partner fall into.

Note: Keep in mind that people can have toxic or healthy relationships as it relates to a thing, place or behavior. For example, if a person is dependent upon a substance, he or she is engaged in a toxic relationship with a drug.

Toxic Relationships	Healthy Relationships
Clouded with deceit	Rooted in honesty and truth
Disrespect demonstrated by one or both	Mutual respect is apparent
Distrustful	Trust and safety are present
Lopsided focus	Well-rounded focus
Drama-based	Drama is limited and acute
Feels draining, confusing, depressing, or shameful	Feels energizing, hopeful, and empowering
Solving problems is avoided and differences are viewed as threatening	Problems addressed openly and differences respected
Sense of entrapment or being controlled and manipulated	Increased sense of freedom
Sexism or hierarchy exists	Partners are equals
Boundaries are difficult to detect or are breached	Appropriate boundaries are respected
Breeds selfishness	Encourages self-respect and selflessness
Decreases well-being	Increases well-being
Fear- or lust-based	Love-based
Hinders or stagnates growth	Fosters and encourages growth

Section

8

Am I Serious About Dealing with My Pornography Problem?

I am not serious if:	I am serious about changing if:
I lie, am evasive, or only disclose information when asked.	I am honest.
I was caught or reported by someone else rather than admitting to or confessing inappropriate behavior.	I am open and willing to talk about what I do, think, and feel.
I pretend or try to convince others that there are no problems, that they are taken care of, or are no big deal.	I am trying to find out what caused my addictions and prevent addictive behavior from happening again.
I am defensive, deny, minimize, rationalize, and blame others in order to avoid dealing with my problems.	I take responsibility for making personal changes.
I want to go back to the way things were before getting caught, rather than improving and growing.	I have made up my own rules for staying out of compulsive sexual behaviors and am following them.
I refuse to attend 12-Step meetings or get a sponsor, and continue to "punish" myself.	I regularly attend 12-Step groups, report to my sponsor, and accept the Atonement in my life.
I am not willing to put in the time or effort to fix problems or work the 12-Steps.	I am working on the 12-Steps and my issues daily.
I run away, hide, or won't talk about my behaviors, feelings, thoughts, and fantasies.	I meet regularly with my ecclesiastical leader.
I do not actively participate in counseling.	I decide to see a counselor on my own rather than being forced to or told to by someone else.
I use other addictions—like alcohol or drugs—to avoid dealing with my real problems.	I go to professional counseling sessions, work on issues underlying my behavior, and do all homework given.
I act as if I am the victim and seek sympathy or try to get others to take sides.	I am working more on what I need to change rather than on what I think my spouse needs to change.
I want my spouse to be okay with my addictions and I feel cheated if I can't continue.	I give my spouse the space and closeness she needs.
I criticize and blame others more than I take personal responsibility.	I show that I understand the hurt which I have caused my spouse and loved ones.
I am angry, moody, resentful, critical, or out of control, and only think about my own needs.	I work to earn others' trust and forgiveness.
I try to make a quick-fix deal and apologize—just to have the issue dropped.	I work to solve problems that were caused by my addiction.
I am manipulative and use fear, guilt, or threats to get what I want.	I speak and act with respect.
I make impulsive decisions and have impulsive behaviors.	I am dependable in taking care of my family, occupation, and religious responsibilities.
I make promises rather than changes.	I am setting specific, measurable goals and achieving them.
I am not living Church standards.	I am living the standards of the Church.
I continue to put myself in situations where I'll be tempted.	I have made significant lifestyle changes.

Am I Making Effective Changes to Deal with My Spouse's Addiction?

I am probably not making needed changes if:	I am making effective changes if:
I feel that in some way my spouse's addiction is my fault and blame myself for his behavior.	I recognize that pornography addiction is a serious problem and requires hard work to find recovery. However, I do not blame myself for my spouse's addiction.
I pretend there isn't a problem, it is already taken care of, or it isn't a big deal.	I require honesty and transparency from the addict and ask him directly when something is bothering me.
I believe whatever the addict tells me, even if my gut tells me something is wrong.	I take responsibility for making positive changes in my life.
I refuse to take responsibility for changing what I can and taking care of myself.	I find help and support from others in dealing with the betrayal and trauma I am experiencing and its impact on me.
I try to deal with my emotions on my own.	I openly share what I think, feel, and am experiencing with appropriate trusted people.
I keep the addiction a secret and fail to seek outside help.	I meet regularly with my ecclesiastical leader.
I think that only the addict needs counseling, not me; or, I fail to do homework and skip sessions.	I work with a therapist who is trained in sexual addiction—whether or not my spouse wants me to.
I make excuses for not attending 12-Step meetings for spouses or, quit going once I feel okay again.	I actively attend 12-Step meetings for spouses and work on my own recovery daily.
I rationalize that I don't really need any guidance.	I find a sponsor and work with her regularly.
I neglect or minimize my needs and wants.	I practice self-care daily.
I bury my emotions, or utilize other addictions such as food or drugs to avoid them.	I allow myself to feel natural emotions, hurt, and anger, and then surrender them to God.
I persist in believing that God doesn't care about me.	I seek to feel God's love for me.
I deny, minimize, rationalize, or blame others to avoid making changes or letting go of resentment.	I work towards forgiving and letting go of the resentment for the hurt which the addicted spouse has caused.
I criticize or blame the addict—rather than set boundaries or make changes to protect myself.	I set and follow boundaries to protect myself from my spouse's addictive behavior and from obsessing about his addiction.
I make a quick-fix deal: If the addict says he is sorry, I will just forget it and won't talk about it anymore.	I refuse to accept or enable addict behavior; I look for positive changes—not just promises.
I obsess about what the addict needs to do, rather than work on my own recovery.	I focus on the changes that I can make, rather than on what I think my spouse needs to change.
I choose how to act based on my fear of the addict's reaction, or I respond explosively.	I appropriately share my needs and feelings with the addict instead of worrying about how he might respond.
I set my level of affection based on what my spouse wants rather than on what I need.	I ask for the space, closeness, or help that I need.
I go along with addictive behavior, or tell myself that it is okay—or that it is not really that bad.	I work towards extending trust if my spouse is showing behavior that is deserving of trust.
I use demands, fear, guilt, manipulation, or threats to get what I want or need.	I take care of my personal and family needs.
I do it all myself—even if I'm overwhelmed, and constantly demand perfection from myself.	I set small measurable goals for myself and work for progr[ess] not perfection.
I do not put in the time and effort to deal with the problem, or fail to set realistic expectations.	I accept that healing from the effects of my spouse's a[ddiction is] a long process that will take time and effort.

Common Terms

90 in 90: Attending 90 12-Step meetings in 90 days as a way to jump-start recovery

Animated pornography: Cartoons that depict pornographic stories or images

Anonymity: The focus in 12-Step fellowships to keep names and information learned in groups confidential

ARP (Addiction Recovery Program): A 12-Step fellowship for all addictions sponsored by LDSFS free of charge

Child pornography: Portrays children or adolescents engaged in sexual activities

Closed meetings: A 12-Step meeting that is only open to those who are seeking personal recovery. Generally SA or S-Anon meetings are closed

Cybersex: Any sexual activity, display, or discussion engaged in by means of a computer

Erotica: Sexually explicit literature or art

Family Support Groups: 12-Step meetings run by LDSFS for the loved ones of addicts

Hard-core pornography: Graphic depictions of sexual acts

Internet pornography: Pornography distributed via the Internet

LDSFS: LDS Family Services

Lust: Uncontrolled or illicit sexual desire or appetite

Masturbation: Stimulating oneself to satisfy sexual urges

Obscenity: The character or quality of being morally offensive

Online sexual activity: When two or more people connected via the Internet send sexually explicit messages as they role play or describe a sexual experience

PASG (Pornography Addiction Support Group): A 12-Step group for those struggling with pornography addiction, sponsored by LDSFS

Pornography: Writing, pictures, or films designed to stimulate sexual excitement

Promiscuity: Sex with many partners

Recovery: Replacing addictive habits with honest, open, and healthy behaviors

SA (Sexaholics Anonymous): A nationally-based 12-Step program, patterned after Alcoholics Anonymous, for those struggling with pornography and sexual addiction

S-Anon: A nationally-based 12-Step program for the loved ones of sexual pornography addicts

Sexting: When an individual sends sexually explicit text messages or pictures to another person

Sobriety: Abstinence from sexual relations with oneself or any partners besides one's spouse

Soft-core pornography: Less graphic pornography including suggestive music videos, swimsuit magazines, sexualized stories, or pictures of partially naked or fully naked people

Sponsor: A person who has recovered from a specific addiction and can offer hope, support, and practical guidance to a recovering addict

Triggers: Stimuli, conflicts, or pressures that provoke a fantasy, feeling, or thought that leads to our acting out

White Book: The guidebook for SA meetings published by SA International

Books about Understanding Pornography and Sexual Addiction *(LDS Perspective)*

- *He Restoreth My Soul: Understanding and Breaking the Chemical and Spiritual Chains of Pornography Addiction Through the Atonement of Jesus Christ* (2010), Donald L. Hilton, Jr., M.D.; Forward Press.

- *Confronting Pornography: A Guide to Prevention and Recovery for Individuals, Loved Ones, and Leaders* (2005), Mark Chamberlain, Dan Gray, & Rory Reid (Editors); Deseret Book.

Books about Understanding Pornography and Sexual Addiction *(General Perspective)*

- *What's the Big Deal about Pornography? A Guide for the Internet Generation* (2008), Jill C. Manning; Shadow Mountain Press (General Audience/Parents and Youth).

- *Out of the Shadows: Understanding Sexual Addiction* (2001), Patrick Carnes; Hazelden.

Books written to the Afflicted Spouse or Loved One of a Pornography and Sexual Addict *(LDS Perspective)*

- *Lord, I Believe; Help Thou Mine Unbelief: A Workbook Approach* (2005), Rod W. Jeppsen.

- *Love You, Hate the Porn: Healing a Relationship Damaged by Virtual Infidelity* (2011), Mark Chamberlain, PhD & Geoff Steurer, MS, LMFT.

- *From Heartache to Healing: Finding Power In Christ to Deal With A Loved One's Sexual Addiction* (2010), Colleen C. & Philip A. Harrison, Windhaven Publishing.

Books written to the Afflicted Spouse or Loved One of a Pornography and Sexual Addict *(General Perspective)*

- *Codependent No More: How to Stop Controlling Others and Start Caring for Yourself*, Melody Beattie; Hazelden.

- *Your Sexually Addicted Spouse: How Partners Can Cope and Heal* (2009), Barbara Steffens & Marsha Means; New Horizon.

Books Relating to 12-Step Programs for the Sexually Addicted

- *Sexaholics Anonymous White Book* (1989), SA Literature. (For Pornography & Sexual Addicts) *www.sa.org*

- *Addiction Recovery Program: A Guide to Addiction Recovery and Healing*, LDS Family Services.

- *He Did Deliver Me from Bondage* (2002), Colleen G. Harrison; Windhaven Publishing and Productions. (LDS).

- *A Gentle Path Through the 12-Steps, The Classic Guide for All People In the Process of Recovery* (1993), Patrick Carnes, Ph.D. Hazelden.

Books Relating to 12-Step Programs for an Afflicted Spouse or Loved One

- *S-Anon 12-Steps*, S-Anon Literature [for the loved ones of sexual addicts] *www.sanon.org*

- *He Did Deliver Me from Bondage* (2002), Colleen G. Harrison; Windhaven Publishing and Productions (LDS perspective).

Resources

Teaching Children about Healthy Sexuality:

- *A Parent's Guide*, see *www.lds.org*

- *Family Home Evening Resource Manual* (1983), (p 253–60).

- *Let Virtue Garnish Thy Thoughts*, LDS Church Distribution.

- *How to Talk to Your Child about Sex* (1999), Linda and Richard Eyre; St. Mark's Press.

- *Growing Up: Gospel Answers about Maturation and Sex* (2000), Brad Wilcox; Deseret Book Company.

- *Where Did I Come From?* (2000), Peter Mayle; Kensington Publishing Corp.

SA Lifeline Materials Available Online
(*www.salifeline.org*)

- *Common Terms*

- *Recovery and Healing from the Effects of Pornography and Sexual Addiction* (**Pamphlet**)

- *Dating and Pornography* (**Pamphlet**)

- *The Family Fight Against Pornography* (**Pamphlet**)

- *Young Single Adult Pledge* (produced by Deseret Media)

- *Family Pledge* (produced by Deseret Media)

- *Contrasting Healthy Sexuality and Pornographic Portrayals of Sexuality* (**Chart by Jill C. Manning, PhD**)

- *Comparing Healthy and Toxic Relationships* (**Chart by Jill C. Manning, PhD**)

- *Am I Serious About Dealing with My Pornography Problem?*

- *Am I Making Effective Changes to Deal with My Spouse's Pornography Problem?*

Internet Sites

- *www.combatingpornography.org*

- *www.salifeline.org*

- *http://www.providentliving.org/familyservices/ AddicitonRecoveryManual_36764000.pdf*

- *www.outinthelight.com*

- *www.rowboatandmarbles.com*

- *www.sa.org*

- *www.sanon.org*

DVDs

- *Out in the Light*, Deseret Media Corporation. (*www.outinthelight.com*)

- *Avoiding/Overcoming Pornography, Real Families Real Answers*. (*www.byutv.org/ watch/1377-113*)

- *Pornography and the Brain*, Dr. Donald L. Hilton Jr., MD. (*www.salifeline.org*)

- *Preparing for Healthy Intimacy: A Message for Singles*, Jill C. Manning, PhD and Dan Gray. (*www.salifeline.org*)

- *Pornography the Great Lie: A Guide for Families of All Faiths*. Deseret Book

- *Healing Relationships Damaged by Pornography*, Geoff Steurer. (*www.salifeline. org*)

- *Safeguarding Teens and Young Adults from Pornography*. Jason Carroll, PhD. (*www. salifeline.org*)

◆ Audio CDs

- ◈ *Strengthening Recovery through Strengthening Marriage*, 6-part Audio Program, Geoff Steurer and Kevin Skinner. For couples dealing with pornography addiction. (order at *www.salifeline.org*)

- ◈ *Let's Talk about the Elephant in the Room*, (2010) Jill C. Manning, PhD, CD *www.deseretbook.com*.

Locating a Therapist

- ◈ Find a Therapist *www.salifeline.org*.

- ◈ LifeSTAR Network *www.lifestarnetwork.org*

- ◈ LDS Hope and Recovery *www.ldshopeandrecovery.com*

- ◈ Arch Counseling *www.archcounseling.com*

- ◈ LDS Family Services *www.providentliving.org*

12-Step Programs / Finding Meetings

- ◈ Sexaholics Anonymous 12-Step Meetings in Utah: *www.salifeline.org*

- ◈ Sexaholics Anonymous 12-Step Meetings outside Utah: *www.sa.org/top*

- ◈ S-Anon 12-Step Meetings in Utah visit *www.salifeline.org*

- ◈ S-Anon 12-Step Meetings outside Utah visit *www.sanon.org*

LDS PASG (Pornography Addiction Support Groups) *and Family Support Groups*

- ◈ *www.providentliving.org/content/list/0,11664,4177-1,00.html*

Internet Filters

- ◈ *www.k9webprotection.com*

- ◈ *www.opendns.com*

Section

9

Bibliography

- *A Parent's Guide*, see The Church of Jesus Christ of Latter-day Saints.

- *Addiction Recovery Program: A Guide to Addiction Recovery and Healing*, LDS Family Services.

- *Chased by an Elephant* (2010), Jamie Barrett Graham, Tidle Wave Books.

- *Clean Hands, Pure Heart* (2010), Phil Harrison, Windhaven Publishing.

- *Codependent No More: How to Stop Controlling Others and Start Caring for Yourself* (1986), Melody Beattie, Hazelden Publishing.

- *Confronting Pornography: A Guide to Prevention and Recovery for Individuals, Loved Ones, and Leaders* (2005), ed. Mark Chamberlain, Dan Gray, & Rory Reid, Deseret Book.

- *Family Home Evening Resource Manual*, 1983, The Church of Jesus Christ of Latter-day Saints, p 253–60.

- *Growing Up: Gospel Answers about Maturation and Sex*, Brad Wilcox, Deseret Book Co.

- *He Did Deliver Me from Bondage* (2002), Colleen Harrison, Windhaven Publishing.

- *He Restoreth My Soul* (2010), Donald L. Hilton, Jr., M.D. Forward Press.

- *How Babies Are Made?* (1984), Andrew Audry and Stephen Schep, Little, Brown & Co.

- *How to Talk to Your Child about Sex* (1999), Linda and Richard Eyre, St. Martin's Press.

- "Let Virtue Garnish Thy Thoughts," pamphlet at LDS Church distribution.

- *Let's Talk about the Elephant in the Room*, Jill C. Manning, PhD.

- *Living with Your Husband's Secret Wars* (1999), Marsha Means. Fleming H. Revell, Grand Rapids, MI.

- *Lord, I Believe: Help Thou Mine Unbelief*, by Rod W. Jeppsen, MC, LPC, CSAT.

- *Out of the Shadows: Understanding Sexual Addiction* (2001), Patrick Carnes. Hazelden.

- *S-Anon: 12-Steps*, S-Anon Literature.

- *Sexaholics Anonymous White Book* (1989), SA Literature.

- *Strengthening Recovery through Strengthening Marriage*, CDs, Geoff Steurer and Kevin Skinner.

- *The Porn Trap* (2010), Wendy Maltz and Larry Maltz, Harper Collins Publishers.

- *To Strengthen the Family*, JoAnn Hamilton.

- *What's the Big Deal about Pornography? A Guide for the Internet Generation* (2008), Jill C. Manning. Shadow Mountain Press.

- *Where Did I Come From?* (2000), Peter Mayle, Kensington Publishing.